LOVE AND SYMPATHY IN THERAVĀDA BUDDHISM

LOVE AND SYMPATHY IN THERAVĀDA BUDDHISM

HARVEY B. ARONSON

MOTILAL BANARSIDASS
Delhi :: Varanasi :: Patna

Indological Publishers and Booksellers
Head Office : 40-U.A., Bungalow Road, Delhi-110 007
Branches : 1. Chowk, Varanasi-1 (U.P.)
2. Ashok Rajpath, Patna-4 (BIHAR)

First Edition : Delhi, 1980

Printed in India
By Shantilal Jain, at Shri Jainendra Press
A-45, Phase-1, Industrial Area, Naraina, New Delhi-110 028
Published by Narendra Prakash Jain, for Motilal Banarsidass,
Bungalow Road, Jawahar Nagar, Delhi-110 007

To :

George and Bessie Aronson

Richard H. Robinson

Satyanarayan Goenka-jii

PREFACE

This work has its earliest roots in my study of works on religious love by Soren Kierkegaard and Martin Buber. A lecture by Dr. Richard Alpert made me aware of complementary material on this and related topics in the Asian religious traditions. My interests eventually became focused on Buddhism under the formal instruction of the graduate faculty at the University of Wisconsin, Madison. There I was guided by Professors Stephan Beyer, Minoru Kiyota, Khentsur Rinbochay Ngawang Legden, Arthur Link, Robert Miller, A. K. Narain, Usha Nilsson, Geshe Lhundup Sopa, and Frances Wilson in the preparations necessary for undertaking this work. I am saddened that my mentor Professor Richard H. Robinson could not live to see this, the revision of my doctoral dissertation, in print. His encouragement to do field work led me to India where my appreciation of Buddhism deepened significantly.

I am grateful to the government of India for allowing me to be a visiting scholar in their country where I was able to complete the initial phases of this study. I am especially indebted to the American Institute of Indian Studies, New Delhi, which arranged and supported my stay in India. At the Institute, Professor Robert Miller and Mr. P. R. Mehendiratta were solicitous of my every need. They arranged for my work to be directed by the kind and helpful Professor Jagannath Upadhyaya of Varanaseya Sanskrit Vishvavidyalaya.

In India Elizabeth Napper informed me about the Theravāda meditation teacher Satyanarayan Goenka-jii and for this I am most grateful. Goenka-jii patiently and joyfully opened my eyes to the riches of Theravāda Buddhism. My appreciation of his teachings has been deepened by my contacts with John Coleman and Robert Hover. In addition I am grateful to Mrs. Nina Van Gorkom whose instructions on the Theravāda analysis of phenomena revealed connections between theory and practice formerly overlooked. Professor Donald Swearer's work on modern Theravāda helped focus my concerns in Theravāda psychology and ethics. Though I have not met the authors, my study of Theravāda has been most influenced by the clear and stimulating works of Ledi Sayadaw, Naṇamoli Thera, Nyanaponika Thera, and Buddhadasa Bhikkhu.

This work would not have been possible without the assistance of the University of Virginia Alderman Library, especially its Interlibrary Loan staff and the altruistic South Asia Bibliographer, Richard Martin. Comments on this study by my colleagues Professors John Roberts and Seshagiri Rao were most beneficial. The findings have been tested and tempered through extensive discussion with Professor David Little whose probing questions helped me formulate the overall analytical framework for this presentation, particularly the last chapter. The encouragement and editorial advice offered by Professor Jeffrey Hopkins during the latter stages of this project is deeply appreciated. The University of Virginia has been most generous in defraying the secretarial expenses incurred during the final preparation of this work.

I would like to thank my friends Davis Dillon and Professor Natalie Maxwell for the fruitful discussion we had on the issues involved in this work, and Leah Zahler and Don Lopez for their stylistic suggestions. Allen and Patsy Howard were most kind to design the book jacket. Finally, I am grateful to Anne C. Klein for her inspiring and sustaining companionship during the wonder filled years in which this work was being completed.

Quotations from Winston King's, *In the Hope of Nibbana* are used by permission of Open Court Publishing Company; from Melford Spiro's *Buddhism and Society*, by permission of Harper and Row, Publishers. The Buddha on the cover is from the Munsterberg collection and is reproduced with the permission of Hugo Munsterberg, New Paltz, New York.

This study was made possible by all those mentioned above as well as the countless individuals who have preserved the Theravāda tradition over numerous centuries. I hope that I have done justice to that tradition and that those who read this work will benefit.

Sabbe sattā sukhitā hontu !
May all beings be happy !

University of Wisconsin
1980

H.B. ARONSON

CONTENTS

INTRODUCTION

In the Theravāda Buddhist discourses Gotama Buddha often tells the monks to cultivate love (*mettā*), or to act out of sympathy (*anukampā*). Our immediate reaction might be that the highest expression of sympathy is to aid others' material well-being, but our esteem for material assistance presupposes that a person has only one life to live and thus our main concern should be to make it pleasurable. Gotama, however, taught that we are actually trapped in a beginningless continuum of rebirth — perpetually re-experiencing the sufferings of birth, old age, sickness, and death. He also taught that the escape from this entrapment is the immortal state called nirvāṇa. His and his disciples' teachings which show the way to end suffering and attain this immortal state are an expression of sympathy for the plight of the world.

This book discusses the context and contents of the Theravāda teachings on love, sympathy, and the collective meditative set of four sublime attitudes (*brahma-vihāra*) — universal love, compassion, sympathetic joy, and equanimity.[1] The presentation is based upon the first four of the five collections of Buddha's discourses,[2] a stylistically homogeneous compilation of the earliest strata of Theravāda scripture compiled before 350 B.C.[3] These come to sixteen volumes in Pali and contain a representative sample of Gotama's teachings on love, sympathy, and the four sublime attitudes. The related Theravāda commentaries are examined. Compiled and translated from Sinhalese into Pali by Buddhaghoṣa in the fifth century A.D.,[4] these texts were composed in India during the first two centuries after Gotama and in Ceylon between the third century B.C. and the second century A.D.[5] Since the Sinhalese works upon which Buddhaghosa based his collection no longer exist,[6] his commentaries are the major source for understanding the elaborate system that constitutes Theravāda Buddhism. (Unless otherwise noted, all commentaries mentioned in this work are those collected and translated by Buddhaghoṣa). Of prime importance also is Buddhaghoṣa's *The Path of Purification* (*Visuddhimagga*),[7] the earliest thorough explanation of the Theravāda system of philosophy, ethics, psychology, and practice extant in Pali.

Traditionally, monks expressed their sympathy to laypeople through education at the village level. This has been replaced to a large extent by modern Christian or state schools. Furthermore, that traditional education, with its emphasis on Pali, Sanskrit, cultural history, and so forth, has little application in civil-service or business careers. Thus, the monastic educational system has lost its appeal and fallen into eclipse, with the result that a pressing problem facing the Buddhist monastic community today is the revitalization of its expression of sympathy for others.

Two modern Western scholars, Winston King and Melford Spiro, have asserted that the normative ethic of Theravāda Buddhism is one of withdrawal from society and abstention from social involvement.[8] According to King and Spiro's view, the current situation of diminished monastic social involvement reflects a supposed ethical norm established in the discourses and their commentaries. However, a rigorous analysis of the specific instructions on social concern — namely, the teachings on love, sympathy, and the sublime attitudes — indicates this is not the case. Furthermore, the historical records indicate that up to the modern period the Buddhist monastic community has been actively involved in improving the community life of the societies where it has flourished.[9] Still, King and Spiro's characterization has achieved such widespread currency and acceptance that many in the West consider it the orthodox interpretation of Theravāda ethics. However, since neither King nor Spiro works in Pali, neither has done the close textual and commentarial work necessary to support their theory. Therefore, after discussing the Pali material relevant to these topics in the first five chapters of this work, I have included a detailed examination and critique of their position in Chapter Six. My concern is with the motives to social action as well as the psychological and soteriological import of the Theravāda teachings on love, sympathy, and the sublime attitudes. Only through seeing these facets can the unique vision of Theravāda Buddhism be appreciated.

CHAPTER ONE

BUDDHA'S SYMPATHY

Gotama Buddha was a sympathetic teacher as is clear from the numerous references to Gotama's sympathy in the Therāvada discourses. Etymologically, "sympathy" (*anukampā*) can be understood as the condition of "being moved" (*kampa*) "in accordance with [others]," or "in response to [others]" (*anu*).[1] Though not defined in Buddha's discourses, there are definitions in the commentaries — "the preliminary level of love" (*mettāya pubbabhāga*, DA.ii.456),[2] or "the state of having a tender mind" (*muducittatā*, SA.ii.169). Similarly, it is said to be synonymous with "tender care" (*anuddayā*, SA.ii.169), and "simple compassion" (*kāruñña*, SA.ii.169).

In the *Gradual Sayings* Buddha says :

> Monks, there is one individual who arose and came to be for the welfare of the multitudes, for the happiness of the multitudes, out of sympathy for the world; for the benefit, welfare, and happiness of gods and humans. Who is that one individual ? The Harmonious One, the Perfectly Enlightened One. (A.i.22)

Gotama's fundamental motive in arising and coming to be was his concern for others' welfare.[3] Four innumerable and a hundred thousand eons ago, the ascetic Sumedha made the vow to train over the course of many lives in order to appear as the individual whom we now know as Gotama Buddha. The period from Sumedha's vow to the moment preceding Gotama's full penetration of the four noble truths was his "arising" (AA.i. 98-99). His liberation from suffering, the result of thorough comprehension of the four noble truths, was his "coming to be."

Out of sympathy,[4] the continuum of individuals from Sumedha up to Gotama cultivated the virtues necessary for the realization of the four noble truths at a time when they were not being taught in the world. Realizing these healing truths and becoming completely free from the anguish associated with greed, hatred, and delusion, the Buddha became a teacher serving a humanity beseiged by gross and subtle forms of suffering.

The beneficiaries of Gotama's kindness were those helped in their religious progress through following his instructions. The range of individuals aided is not, however, limited to those present for his teaching. Rather, all those "until now, and those from now into the future, who establish themselves in the paths, fruitions, and heavens depending on the teaching" are the beneficiaries (AA.i.101).

Practitioners who depend on Buddha's instructions can experience the four paths and fruitions. The four paths are brief but decisive stages in realizing or becoming conscious of nirvāṇa. With each successive realization, the practitioner deepens an understanding of the supramundane reality, nirvāṇa. As his comprehension of the changeless deepens, his entanglement with the world of changing phenomena weakens. At each of the four stages, he forever abandons entangling defilements that would otherwise bind him to continuous rebirth and all its attendant sufferings (Vism.xxii.47-77).

Immediately following the experience of each path, the practitioner enjoys the fruition of the path—a short continuation of the realization of nirvāṇa, conjoined with an enjoyment of the new-found freedom from the defilements that have been abandoned. An individual who has traversed all four paths and experienced all four fruitions is called a Worthy One (*Arahant*). Liberated from all mental defilement and free from all future rebirth, at death he is freed from all worldly phenomena in the ultimate security of nirvāṇa.

Even a person who experiences the first path makes a decisive step toward liberation, for after a maximum of seven rebirths among gods and humans he becomes free from all rebirth, in the peace of nirvāṇa (Vism.xxii.18). With the experience of the first path he enters the stream that leads to nirvāṇa and is, therefore, called a Stream-Enterer. Even a conscientious practitioner who fails to achieve this state will achieve rebirth in a heaven after death. Thus, the beneficial results of Buddha's teaching are considerable.

Gotama was similarly concerned for the good fortune of other beings :

> He came to be for the benefit, welfare, and happiness not only of gods and humans but also for the remaining beings, such as snakes, well-winged birds, and so forth. This [phrase "gods and humans"] is said to show those individuals who are fit to realize the paths and fruits [because] they have rebirth endowed with [the proper] conditions. Therefore, it should be understood that he arose for the sake of the happiness, welfare, and profit of these [other beings] as well. (AA.i.101)

The beneficiaries of Buddha's benevolence include the multitudes of species over a vast period of time. For example, it is said that once a frog was sitting in the vicinity of Buddha when he was preaching. A farmer accidentally impaled the frog with his staff, but the frog, through merely hearing the Buddha's voice, had accumulated sufficient merit to be reborn in a heaven. He was able to visit the Buddha from there, receive instruction, and achieve the first supramundane stage of realization, that of Stream-Enterer (Vism.vii.51).

A further interpretation :

> *For the welfare of the multitudes* means that being endowed with wisdom, he instructs [others] with regard to benefits [to be obtained] in this life and that to come. *For the happiness of the multitudes* means that being endowed with an open hand, he shows the happiness of service. *Out of sympathy for the world* means that being endowed with love and compassion, he guards and protects the world like a parent. *For the benefit, welfare, and happiness of gods and humans* : it should be understood that by mentioning humans and gods in this [statement], he includes only individuals who are fit — that is to say, tractable sentient beings. He teaches about his own coming to be so that they may attain the paths, fruitions, and nirvāṇa [by following his example]. *For the benefit* means for the sake of the ultimate aim, for the sake of nirvāṇa. *For the welfare* means for the sake of the path that leads to it, since there is no welfare superior to the path that leads to nirvana. *For the happiness* means for the sake of the fruition-attainment,[5] since there is no happiness superior to this. (MA.i.123)

Buddha arose and came to be out of sympathy for the world that can be compared to the concern of a parent for a child. Fueling the training for Buddhahood, this led Gotama to guard and protect others from suffering by showing them the way to become free from it — teaching them the paths, fruitions, and nirvāṇa.[6]

Buddha's motive for teaching others was a very special kind of sympathy. He was neither overcome nor bound by it. In the *Kindred Sayings* Gotama makes this point to the spirit Sakka :

> Sakka, a wise individual would not sympathize [with others] out of the same motives which bring others together.
>
> If one with a clear mind instructs another, he is not bound through it, by his sympathy, or by his tender care. (S.i.206)

The bonds of fondness and attachment that bring worldly individuals together influence their sympathy. However, Gotama's interest in others' happiness was free from all normal worldly bias and attachment, and, thus, it was unbound. He was not fettered by helping others progress.

Similarly, Gotama was not motivated by considerations of personal gain but was concerned solely with the well-being of his audience. In the *Kindred Sayings* the deity Māra, the embodiment of sense desire,[7] tries to perplex Gotama and induce him to stop teaching (S.i.111). Māra tries to appeal to Gotama's own values to persuade him. He tells the teacher to give up teaching, as it must involve him in a desirous bias and dissatisfaction. Gotama answers Māra's request :

> The Harmonious One is sympathetic
> To others' welfare, he is enlightened.
> When he teaches, he is liberated
> From [desirous] bias and dissatisfaction. (S.i.111)

To those who might object that action is impossible without desire, the Theravāda tradition answers with a subtle psychological analysis of the nature of desirous and wholesome states of mind.

Sense-desire (*kāma*) and attachment (*lobha*) are unwholesome and lead into increasingly intense involvement with misguided habituation. This causes repeated birth with all the suffering it entails. Attachment is an attitude of the mind that grasps an object and sticks to it as meat sticks to a hot frying pan (Vism. xiv.162). It always occurs in association with delusion, agitation, lack of conscience, and lack of shame (Vism.xiv.159-69). Delusion is lack of clarity regarding the true nature of things (Vism.xiv.162) and agitation is mental disquiet (Vism.xiv.165). Conscience and shame — the absence of which characterizes attachment — are the abandonment of erroneous ways out of concern for oneself and others respectively (Vism.xiv.142). Attachment always occurs with a lack of clarity, a lack of mental peace, and a disregard for what is most helpful to oneself and others.

Absence of attachment does not preclude action, for every wholesome state of mind is free of it. There are attitudes, or mental factors (*cetasika*), that occur in a wholesome mind and serve to motivate, or facilitate, wholesome activity. According to *The Path of Purification*, these are intention, concentration, initial application of the mind to an object, sustained application of the mind to an object, energy, inclination to act, decision, flexibility, adaptability, proficiency, abstention from wrong activity, abstention from wrong speech, and abstention from wrong livelihood (Vism.xiv.133-56).[8] None of these is described in the same way as attachment. Though the functions of a few seem close to the function of the latter, there are distinct and fundamental differences as will be explained later.[9] Because it is possible to act without attachment, it was possible for Gotama to teach others and yet be free from bias and ensnarement. Rather than give up consideration of the world's welfare, Buddha maintained a refined and purified concern that was free from all taint. His balanced involvement was a model for his disciples, from beginners to the fully enlightened Worthy Ones.

Gotama's interest in others' success not only motivated him to teach, but also led him to undertake a specific course of conduct. In the "Discourse on Fear and Terror" Gotama tells the Brahmin Jānussoni that he lives in the forest not just because it is pleasant but also out of sympathy for the people of the future (M.i.23; see also A.i.60). For, in the future, sons of good family would consider that Gotama, who had nothing left to accomplish, nevertheless continued to live in the forest whereby they would not be able to find an excuse for giving up this practice. Living in the forest, they would quickly make an end to suffering (MA.i. 129). Buddha lived apart from the confluence of society intent on helping the members of society. He showed others a better way of living through example.

It is related that even when Gotama was grievously pained by a potsherd splinter and lay down, he remained sympathetic to all living beings (S.i.110). Though Gotama experienced *physical* pain, he was able to maintain a benevolent mind.[10] His mind was strong; his kindness, durable.

Timeliness of Buddha's Sympathy

In the "Discourse with Prince Abhaya," the Jain leader Nātaputta recruits Prince Abhaya to put a dilemma to the Buddha (M.i.392-95). Prince Abhaya is told to ask whether Buddha will say things that are not pleasing to others. If Buddha answers yes, then he can be asked to explain how he differs from worldly people. If he answers no, then he can be asked to explain his earlier prediction that his villainous cousin Devadatta will go to hell when he dies, since this was unpleasant to Devadatta.[11]

Abhaya goes to Gotama and asks Nātaputta's question. Buddha replies, "There is no certainty with regard to this" (M.i.393). Using an example, he asks the prince what he would do if his son took a wooden chip or a potsherd and put it into his mouth. The prince replies that if he could not get it out easily, he would get it out even if he had to draw blood, because he has sympathy for his son.

Buddha explains that it is the same with regard to his speech. He does not say what is untrue, profitless, and unpleasant, nor what is true, profitless, and unpleasant. On the other hand, he knows the right time to say things that are true and profitable, yet are unpleasant. Similarly, he does not say what is untrue, profitless and pleasant, nor what is true, profitless and pleasant, but he knows the right time to say things that are true, profitable, and pleasant. Gotama states that his sympathy for all beings motivates him to true and profitable speech. Just as a father, attentive to his son's health, will remove a potsherd from his son's mouth even if he has to draw blood, so, too, Buddha speaks to others, attentive to their benefit, even if the words are not pleasant. Concerned regard motivates his speech, which is reliable, helpful, and timely but not necessarily pleasant. Buddha's prediction concerning Devadatta conformed to these criteria.

Receiving Gifts out of Sympathy

In the *Kindred Sayings*, the Jain Nātaputta recruits a village headman to put a difficult question to Gotama (S.iv.322-25) : Inasmuch as Buddha praises care, protection, and sympathy for the people, how is it that he persists in going for alms with a great company of monks in drought-stricken Nālanda? The village headman, Asibandhakaputta, goes and asks the question, to which Buddha answers that he can remember back ninety-one aeons and does not know of one family that had been harmed by giving alms.[12]

Gotama explains that all families who have wealth, riches, and so on, achieve this status because of gift-giving, truth, and restraint [most likely in a past life]. He also states that the eight sources of harm to a family are a ruler, thief, fire, flood, not obtaining what has been set aside [in storage], becoming misguided and giving up work, a destroyer of the family arising within it, and impermanence.

According to this teaching, giving yields wealth and so forth in return. If harm comes to a family, it does not arise from giving but from one of the eight actual causes of harm. Gotama's answer implies that by allowing others to give alms he was establishing a situation wherein they could create the causes for wealth and riches in the future. Thus, his going for alms and receiving donations, even in a drought-stricken area, is consonant with emphasizing sympathy for the people.

The message of this discourse is harmonious with the teachings in other discourses, which state that giving leads to favorable consequences. In the *Gradual Sayings* Buddha praises alms-giving, especially to Worthy Ones, saying, "He who gives pleasing things [to Worthy Ones] receives pleasing things" (A.iii.49). A Worthy One, in accepting pleasing donations, would be sympathetic to the donor, for he is affording the donor an opportunity to create a pleasurable future. It is recorded that individuals asked Buddha to accept gifts "out of sympathy' (A.iii.49).

In addition to the future benefits of generosity, there are immediate gains as well. Generosity is associated with a wholesome mind,[13] and though one might not have a wholesome mind during every moment of an act of almsgiving, one would for some moments. Since a wholesome mind is associated with the feeling of either happiness or equanimity (Vism.xiv.84) and is completely devoid of mental suffering, an individual who naturally maintains or makes efforts to maintain the wholesome mind associated with acts of generosity benefits immediately. He experiences the satisfaction of freedom from mental suffering and the ease of equanimity or mental pleasure. Buddha, in going for alms, created a situation in which individuals could enjoy the immediate satisfaction of a wholesome mind while creating the causes for a pleasurable future.

CHAPTER TWO

DISCIPLES' SYMPATHY

In addition to the picture of Gotama's sympathy presented in the discourses, there are a few instances when specific disciples' kindness is singled out for mention. Gotama praises Mahākassapa because he teaches others out of simple compassion, tender care, and sympathy (S.ii.199-200).[1] The commentary indicates that these three fraternal attitudes are similar in that :

> *Tender care* is the condition of protecting another.
> *Sympathy* is the state of having a tender mind.
> Both are the same as simple compassion. (SA.ii.169)

Mahākassapa himself states that he undertook many activities out of sympathy for people in the future : becoming a monk, living in the forest, wearing rags, being contented, living alone, and acting with energy (S.ii.202). It is clear that Mahākassapa, like Buddha, considered himself to be an exemplar who undertook beneficial activities with the hope that others would follow him and benefit similarly. Though Mahākassapa renounced life in society, he did not renounce concern for society. In fact, his renunciatory life was determined by a wish to be a guiding light to others. Furthermore, though he lived apart from society, he actively engaged in helping others through teaching them.

Laypersons, such as Nākula's mother, were also commended for their benevolence (A.iii.295-98). At one time, Nākula's father was seriously ill. His wife advised him not to die with reservations in his mind concerning her, since such a death would be unpleasant. She reassured him that she could support herself, would be loyal to him, would continue to see Buddha and the spiritual community, would maintain correct conduct, was accomplished in calming her mind, and was firmly established in her practice. The commentary explains that Nākula's mother uttered the first three assurances as healing truths (AA.iii.349) since the enunciation of truth was expected to effect physical recuperation. Indeed, her husband became calm and assured, and proceeded to recover from his illness. Subsequently, the couple visited Gotama, who told Nākula's father that he was lucky to have a wife who could advise him and was sympathetic to him.

Monks in general are also said to be sympathetic. They renounce all weapons and "live with sympathy for the welfare of all living and breathing beings" (D.i.63). This virtue is also mentioned in connection with those monks cultivating the concentrated states of absorption in general, as well as those specifically cultivating the concentrated sublime attitudes of love, compassion, sympathetic joy, and equanimity (D.i.71, 250). As part of their preparation, such monks, in addition to renouncing weapons, give up anger and when they succeed in doing this their sympathy receives special mention. Thus, their forsaking weapons and anger, thereby restraining negative actions and attitudes, is seen as one component of their sympathy since it is helpful to others.

Kindness motivates the monks to specific courses of action. In the "Advice to Siṅgāla Discourse" Buddha tells the householder Siṅgāla that a householder should attend to wanderers (*samaṇa*) and Brahmins (*brāhmaṇa*) in five ways and that the latter, in turn, should sympathize with householders in six ways (D.iii.191). ("Wanderer" generally refers to an individual who has renounced the householder's life for a life of wandering, but in more restricted usage it can refer to a Buddhist monk [D.i. 60, 62]. "Brahmin" generally refers to a member of the priestly caste, but can refer to a Worthy One. Here, "wanderers and Brahmins" refer to Buddhist monks [DA.iii.917, 957].) Gotama tells Siṅgāla that householders should attend to wanderers and Brahmins with loving physical, verbal, and mental activities, by keeping their doors open, and by providing material sustenance.[2] Wanderers and Brahmins thus attended will sympathize with a householder in six ways : they will turn the householder away from evil, establish him in auspicious practices, sympathize with him through kindness, cause him to hear what he had not heard before, clarify what he had heard before, and teach him the path to heaven. This discourse indicates that wanderers and Brahmins kindly respond to householders' loving activities by paying specific attention to their past experiences as well as present needs and advising them accordingly. In general, wanderers and Brahmins teach householders the way to heaven because laypersons are usually interested in attaining such rebirth.

The commentary explains how monks sympathize with the householders :

> *They sympathize with him through kindness* by relating [with an all-inclusive wish for others' welfare] in the following way : 'May all sentient beings be happy, free from illness, and free from trouble.' In addition, when they gather fellow religious practitioners who are endowed with correct conduct and go to the home of those who attend to them, they are said to be sympathizing [with their patrons through kindness]. (DA.iii.957).

Monks are benevolent to householders by including them in their all-embracing wish for others' welfare as well as by bringing along fellow monks in their visits. The monks will either receive alms or offer helpful religious instruction. As has been explained above (see above, pp. 9-10), such activities are expressions of kindness, for the monks who facilitate householders' participation in wholesome activities are showing their sympathy for the householders.

Specific activities through which monks express their interest in others' well-being are mentioned in the *Gradual Sayings*. Gotama lists five practices by which monks are sympathetic to laypersons : establishing them in correct conduct; bringing them to a religious outlook; inspiring them to practice mindfulness when they are sick; announcing to them the arrival of monks and thus making them aware of the opportunity to create merit; and eating whatever food they donate and thus not frustrating their gifts of confidence. Both in the "Advice to Siṅgāla," discussed above, and here Gotama is describing the conduct of the monks, implicitly prescribing that such conduct continue.

Expression of kindness involves monks in making a choice of who should be the beneficiaries of their fraternal activity. The grounds for this choice are discussed in the *Gradual Sayings* when General Sīha asks Gotama to teach him the manifest fruits of almsgiving (A.iv.79-81). Gotama asks Sīha to imagine two people, one lacking confidence in the teaching, selfish, hardened, and abusive; the other confident in the teaching, generous, and delighting in almsgiving. He asks Sīha which of these people would first receive the sympathy of the Worthy Ones. Sīha says that the Worthy Ones would first be heedful of the person who has confidence in the teaching, is generous, and delights in almsgiving. Sīha adds that he not only has confidence in this answer but knows from his own experience that this is a manifest fruit of almsgiving.

The commentary explains the responsive sympathy of Worthy Ones : "*Sympathetic*, sympathizing in their minds in this way : 'Whom should we help today ? From whom should we accept alms ? To whom should we teach religion ?' " (AA.iv.40) Taking cognizance of the attitudes and interests of laypersons and trying to maximize the help they can afford, Worthy Ones give preference to receiving alms from and teaching those who are interested in giving alms and being taught.

Teaching others out of Sympathy

In the *Kindred Sayings* Gotama sends the monks out to teach others :

> Monks, go and travel around for the welfare of the multitudes, for the happiness of the multitudes, out of sympathy for the world, for the benefit, welfare, and happiness of gods and humans. Two should not go on one [path]. Monks, teach the dharma that is beneficial in the beginning, beneficial in the middle, and beneficial in the end. (S.i.105)

To motivate the monks to go out and teach others, Gotama uses the same words and phrases he used in describing his own motivation for arising and coming to be (see p. 3).

Gotama does not use the terms "love" (*mettā*) or "compassion" (*karuṇā*) to motivate the monks to teach others, or to describe his own motivation. In the first four collections of discourses, Gotama hardly ever uses the terms "love" or "compassion" in connection with himself, mentioning once his ability to cultivate the four sublime attitudes of love, compassion, sympathetic joy (*muditā*), and equanimity (*upekkhā*) (A.i.180-85) and once that he lives with these attitudes (M.i.368-71). There are also three instances in which terms etymologically related to "compassion" are used in connection with Gotama,[3] but except in these five instances, the terms "love," "compassion," and "sympathetic joy" do not occur in connection with his descriptions of himself, nor are these specific terms, or their etymological relatives, used when he motivates the monks to live a life of itinerant teaching. However, he uses the term "sympathy" and its etymological relatives at least twenty times in connection with himself[4] as in describing his motivation for arising and coming to be. He also uses it to motivate the monks to go out and teach others. The distinctive use of "sympathy," to the exclusion of "love" and "compassion," is especially striking upon considering its semantic relation to the latter terms. Why are these semantically related terms kept doctrinally apart ? To answer this question it is necessary to investigate the level of concentration associated with love, compassion, and sympathy as well as the respective usage of each of these terms.

Love is cultivated at three levels (AA.i.70; see below, p. 25), the most concentrated form occurs at the level of placement concentration (*appanā-samādhi*) in the absorption states (*jhāna*), during which the mind and its associated mental factors are firmly placed on their object (P.P.iii.nt.4). Love at this level is called "placement love."

The second form occurs at the level of access concentration (*upacāra-samādhi*), which occurs immediately preceding absorption and serves as an access to it (Vism.iv.74). Love at this level is called "access love." Since access concentration is also said to be "preliminary" to placement concentration,[5] it can be inferred that love at this level of concentration might also be called "the preliminary level of love."

The third, least concentrated, form of love consists of relating to sentient beings with a wish for their welfare — this being a state not associated with any significant type of concentration. It is considered to be "the rudimentary level of love" (*mettāya sabbapubbabhāga* AA.i.70), but it also is called "the preliminary level of love" (*mettāpubbabhāga* AA.i.70). (When the commentary explains that sympathy is the preliminary level of love [above, p. 3], it could be referring to the second or third types of love).

Though a similar tripartite division of compassion does not occur in the commentaries, such a division is probably founded.

Whereas love — no matter what strength — is epitomized by the wish that all sentient beings be happy, compassion is epitomized with the corresponding wish that they be free from suffering (Pa.ii.128).

At the rudimentary level, the wish itself is the only noteworthy characteristic of love or compassion, but at more profound levels of cultivation love and compassion are specifically characterized by the levels of concentration at which they occur. Also, though in theory love or compassion can occur at three different levels, the usage of the terms in the discourses and their explication in the commentaries indicate that just access or placement love or compassion are intended.[6] "Love" and "compassion" are always qualified by epithets, or by contexts that indicate these two specific strengths; thus, they can be considered technical terms.

Whereas the meanings of "love" and "compassion" are strictly differentiated in the commentaries, the meaning of "sympathy" is diffuse.[7] The strength of sympathy is identified only once as being of the "preliminary level" (DA.ii.456)[8] and is not otherwise qualified to indicate a specific strength of mind. "Sympathy" is a general, not a technical term.

The teachings on sympathy are distinct from the teachings on love and compassion because the latter are meditative topics specifically referring to access or placement states. "Sympathy" never occurs as the prominent term in a discourse concerning meditation,[9] nor is it the object of the verb "cultivate" (*bhāveti*), as in instructions on meditation. Sympathy is the fraternal concern that is present in an individual and does not require cultivation or meditative development. Gotama's audience required no experience in meditation to have a sense of this attitude. In the discourses, "sympathy" is often used by the laymen in the common phrase "out of sympathy" (*anukampam upādāya*), which is used much like our English "kindly."[10] There is no equivalent phrase, in frequency or meaning, involving love or compassion.

Gotama used the non-technical easily understood term "sympathy" and the similarly simple phrases "for the welfare of the multitudes," "for the happiness of the multitudes," in describing his own fundamental motivation and in prescribing others' activities, for if he had used meditative terms, then those monks or laymen with little or no meditative experience or ability might have felt closed off from the religious life. Appealing to his audiences' sympathy he needed no further justification. By using these easy-to-experience and easy-to-understand words and phrases, Gotama increased the likelihood of generating such attitudes in his audience.

In several discourses, Gotama says that monks should help friends and relatives, for whom they feel sympathy, by teaching them the four establishments of mindfulness (S.v.189) and the four noble truths (S.v.434), guiding them until they become Stream-Enterers (S.v.364-65; A.i.222). The most important expression of the monks' sympathy is their teaching.

Sympathy and Practice

Without referring to a higher abstract principle or to reward — immediate or distant — Gotama exhorted his audiences to undertake religious activities by appealing to their sympathy. Sympathy precedes and sustains mental cultivation, not vice versa. During his last stay at Vesāli, Buddha urged the monks to cultivate the practices necessary for direct knowledge of nirvāṇa :

> . . . Monks, you should carefully assume those practices which I have taught for the sake of direct knowledge. You should practice them, cultivate them, and make much of them, so that this religious practice will last for a long time, will be long standing. This is for the welfare of the multitudes, the happiness of the multitudes, the benefit, welfare, and happiness of gods and humans. This is out of sympathy with the world. (D.ii.119)

The monks should take up practices that lead to direct knowledge of nirvāṇa — their continuous cultivation and transmission leading to the perpetuation of the religion, a reflection of the monks' interest in others' welfare. Monks who assume these beneficial practices help themselves. They should, moreover, have the intention of exemplifying the inspiring conduct associated with practice and effectively transmitting the religion to others. This intention, in turn, should arise out of their concern for the world.

The word "monk,' in general, means an individual who has

taken up practice according to Buddha's instructions (DA.iii.755), and thus the above exhortation for monks to practice intent on others' benefit applies to all practitioners — laypeople, monks, and nuns. Practitioners can devote themselves to their own meditative practice and become exemplars of the meditative life — illustrating the conduct and contentment that comes from the eremetic type of life. Or, they can concentrate on teaching morality, philosophy, or meditation. They proportion their commitment to these two equally valid expressions of sympathy, sequentially or simultaneously, in accordance with their teachers' advice, their temperament, and their patrons' needs.

The monks are also instructed to maintain unanimity with regard to the content of the dharma out of concern for others. In the *Dialogues of the Buddha*, Gotama instructs the novice Cunda that the monks should not quarrel over what he has taught, but agree to the form and content of the teaching (D.iii.127).[11] If they do, then the religious doctrine will endure and benefit many. In a harmonious atmosphere monks can proceed with their own exemplary spiritual development and their helpful instruction of others.

Sympathy as Antidote

In the *Gradual Sayings* Sāriputta instructs the monks on how to eliminate hostility that might arise toward others (A.iii.186-90). He enumerates five types of individuals who might be recipients of hostility :

1. those with impure physical activities but pure verbal ones
2. those with pure physical but impure verbal ones
3. those whose physical and verbal activities are impure but who achieve openness of mind and clarity of mind from time to time[12]
4. those whose physical and verbal activities are impure and who do not achieve openness of mind and clarity of mind from time to time.
5. those whose physical and verbal activities are pure and who achieve openness of mind and clarity of mind from time to time.

Sāriputta advises the monks to overcome hostility toward individuals in any of the above-mentioned groups but the fourth by giving attention to the individuals' pure characteristics.

In this technique a practitioner tries to call to mind the pure physical, verbal, or mental activities that have been performed by the current recipient of his hostility (Vism.ix.16-19). Through this, mindfulness and absence of hatred arise, and one's mind becomes clarified with regard to the person. Due to this mindfulness, absence of hatred, and clarity, the practitioner has a wholesome mind.[13] Since an individual cannot have a wholesome and an unwholesome mind at the very same time,[14] establishing a wholesome mind displaces the unwholesomeness.

In practice, one makes the reflection on others' purity familiar by day-to-day repetition, even when one does not feel hostility, for it is of utmost importance that the practitioner experience the full emotive impact of these reflections in the quiet circumstances of daily practice.[15] These reflections must not become empty verbalizations with no personal effect — mere distractions, as it were. When one actually becomes hostile, one then tries to call to mind a pure activity that the other person has performed.

In the initial stages of practice, when one's anger is strong and the emotive force of reflection is weak, it often seems that one is failing. It may appear as if reflection has no power, that it has become a futile thought. Nevertheless, if one can maintain the mind on even the mere verbalization of one's reflections in the heat of a hostile situation, one is training in strengthening mindfulness;[16] it is not that one is having no effect at all in countering hostility. The few moments of mindfulness interspersed in the continuum of anger serve to dispel the anger, and the present moments of mindfulness serve as the causes for deepened mindfulness in the future. Gentle persistence and a tolerance for apparent failure must be maintained. Eventually, one is able to displace anger totally, whereupon one experiences the emotional satisfaction associated with a wholesome mind. The feelings of either equanimity or mental pleasure are enjoyed (Vism.xi.83); body and mind become tranquil, light, flexible and efficient (Vism.xiv.133, 144-49; PP.xiv.nt.65), and one is temporarily free from the mental suffering associated with aversion (Vism.xiv.92). In addition, one is creating the causes and conditions for satisfactory states of mind in the future (P.P.xiv.nt.35).[17] Thus, reflection on another's positive qualities is a method for consciously abandoning anger which, when practiced correctly, does not result in physical or mental suffering.

It stands as a challenge to those who assert that constraint of unwholesome attitudes necessarily leads to mental or physical damage.

Sāriputta urges the monks to eliminate hostility to individuals in the fourth group mentioned above by "establishing" (*upaṭṭhāpetabba*) "simple compassion" (*kāruñña*), "tender care" (*anudayā*), and sympathy for them. *Kāruñña* is never qualified or contextualized in the discourses or commentaries in a way that would indicate that it is a meditative term associated with a specific, cultivated level of concentration.[16] It is not a technical term. Thus, the translation equivalent "simple compassion" has been chosen for it. ("Tender care" is also not a technical term.[19])

The method for removing hostility by establishing compassion, tender care, and sympathy is much the same as that of paying attention to others' purity. One first alternates and ultimately replaces the unwholesome hostile mind with a wholesome one endowed with simple compassion, tender care, or sympathy. Success is gained only if application of the technique becomes habitual. One regularly calls to mind individuals toward whom one feels hostile and methodically establishes the suggested antidotes of simple compassion, and so forth. Sāriputta explains the reflections that are useful for establishing these :

> Friends, it is like this. An ill, suffering, very sick person is on a long road. There are villages far off in front and behind him. He has no suitable food, suitable medicine, suitable servant, nor a guide to the village. Another person on the long road might see and establish simple compassion, tender care, and sympathy for that sick person with the thought :
>
> > May this person obtain suitable food, suitable medicine, a suitable servant, and a guide to the village. Why ? So that this person may be free from misfortune and misery at this time.
>
> Friends, it is similar with regard to an individual with impure physical and verbal activities who does not obtain openness of mind and clarity of mind from time to time. Friends, simple compassion, tender care, and sympathy should be established with regard to such an individual by means of the thought :

> May this respectable individual abandon improper physical activities and cultivate proper ones. May he abandon improper verbal activities and cultivate proper ones. May he abandon improper mental activities and cultivate proper ones. Why ? So that this respectable individual will not be reborn in a state of loss, in a bad fate, in ruin, or in hell after dissolution of the body and death.

In this way hostility is eliminated with regard to that individual. (A.iii.189)

The commentary elaborates on the above analogy :

> *Friends, it is similar* : with regard to this [analogy], the individual who is completely endowed with dark qualities is like the sick and helpless individual. Beginningless cyclic existence is like the long road. The distance to nirvāṇa is like the distance to the villages in front and in back [of the sick individual]. Not enjoying the fruits of being a recluse is like not obtaining proper food. The lack of serenity and insight is like not obtaining proper medicine. The lack of physicians for the [mental] defilements with teachings and instructions is like not obtaining a suitable servant. The condition of not having met the Harmonious One, or a disciple of the Harmonious One, who could lead [the individual] to nirvāṇa is like not obtaining a guide to the village. The individual who lives with love and cools off his mind [if hostility arises toward a totally impure individual] by establishing simple compassion, [tender care, and sympathy] for him is like one who establishes simple compassion, [tender care, and sympathy] when he sees a [sick] person. (AA.iii.297)

The commentary singles out individuals living with love as the specific beneficiaries of these instructions, which are mentioned in *The Path of Purification* as one of the ways a practitioner can abandon hostility if it arises when he is trying to cultivate universal love at the level of absorption (Vism.ix.20). It should be understood, though, that all practitioners can benefit from this technique.

This discourse is unique in that it is the only one in which the audience is called upon to "establish" sympathy. In all other instances, if there is an appeal to sympathy, it is to one that is already there. Furthermore, this is the only discourse in which personal benefit is ascribed to sympathy — namely, the ability to displace hostility. However, as seen above (see above p. 17) sympathy in general needed no justification; its value was implicit.

Simple Compassion and its Function

The term "simple compassion" is so similar to the term "sympathy" in both meaning and usage that in two discourses the two are used synonymously (S.ii.199-200; A.iii.186-90). "Simple compassion" refers to the concern that others be free from suffering and is not restricted to any specific level of concentration, differing from "sympathy" in that it is used far less often in the first four collections of discourses, where it appears only five times.[20] One of these, which appears in the *Gradual Sayings*, shows the necessity for the contextualization of one's responses to others. It points out that on certain occasions an individual is duty bound to intervene on behalf of others' welfare. Gotama's cousin, the monk Ānanda, remains silent when the monk Udāyin stubbornly and erroneously contradicts the more learned Sāriputta on a point of doctrine (A.iii.192-96). When the matter is brought to Gotama's attention, he corrects Udāyin and says to Ānanda :

> Ānanda, will you look on (*ajjhupekkhissatha*) when an elder monk is being bothered ? Will there be no simple compassion (*kāruñña*) [in you] for an elder monk who is being bothered? (A.iii.194)

The commentary states :

> With regard to this, the meaning is : "Ānanda, I do not approve or accept the fact that you look on when an elder monk is bothered." Why did the Fortunate One speak in this way just to the Elder Ānanda ? Because Ānanda was the dharma-treasure-guard. It is the dharma-treasure-guard's duty to control an individual who speaks in that way. Also, this was his duty just because he was the Elder Sāriputta's companion. In this context, it should

> be understood that whatever the Fortunate One said in this way to reproach Ānanda was not just to him but to all the individuals who were present as well. (AA.iii.298-99)

Gotama counseled all that they had a responsibility to intervene when they saw someone acting like Udāyin.

This instruction, together with the considerable material on sympathy, clearly contradicts those who would assert that Theravāda doctrine counsels individuals to turn away from others in thought and deed. Though Gotama advised people to give up unwholesome involvement with others through attachment or hatred, he prescribed wholesome concern and activity for others.

Context is the key to understanding what attitude or response is most appropriate in any given situation. In some, non-intervention and maintenance of a balanced mind constitute the wisest course of action. In the " 'What ?' Discourse" Gotama instructs the monks on what to do if they see a monk who is acting contrary to the rules of training (M.ii.241-42). He advises them not to be hasty in correcting, but to consider the situation carefully. It may or may not be a discomfort to correct the other monk, and he may or may not get angry when corrected, but if a monk is capable of establishing another in wholesomeness (*kusala*), then it is fitting to speak to him. If he would be discomforted in correcting the errant monk and the latter would get angry while not changing his ways, then he should not forget equanimity and remain silent.

The commentary elaborates :

> A monk who sees such an individual urinating while standing and says, "Sir, shouldn't you be sitting ?" is said to have forgotten equanimity. (MA.iv.31)

One of the monks' rules is that unless ill they should not urinate while standing.[21] Clearly someone who cannot keep this simple rule is beyond the pale and does not merit energetic advice; here, it is best to maintain the balance of equanimity.[22]

Chapter Three

LOVING

The Loving Mind

"Love" (*mettā*) is epitomized by the heartfelt wish, "May all beings be happy" (Pa.ii.128). In addition to instructions involving the noun "love" (*mettā*), the discourses contain teachings on the adjective "loving" (*metta*). The topics associated with each are sufficiently distinct to warrant separate consideration. Statements about the one do not necessarily apply to the other.

In the "Smaller Discourse on the Snap of the Fingers" Gotama tells the monks that one who sustains a loving mind (*mettacitta*) for even the duration of a snap of the fingers is called a monk (*bhikkhu*) (A.i.10). Buddha adds that the same is true of a monk who cultivates (*bhāveti*), or pays attention to, a loving mind for the duration of a snap of the fingers. Gotama explains that such a monk's absorption is not in vain; for he is fulfilling the instructions and unwastefully "consuming" (*bhuñjati*) the food of the kingdom (A.i.110).

The commentary to the "Smaller Snap" explains that this discourse was given as a sequel to the "Discourse on the Comparison with a Blaze of Fire" (AA.i.69-70). In the "Blaze of Fire," Gotama teaches the monks that it would be better to endure the blaze of fire, or other assorted sufferings, than to partake of the company of women or to "enjoy" (*paribhuñjeyya*) food and robes (A.iv.128-35). If burned in fire, a monk will suffer for a while or, at the worst, die. If, however, he partakes of the company of a woman or "enjoys" his food and robes, he will be reborn in a hell and experience long-lasting suffering. Using other similarly vivid examples, Gotama concludes by informing the monks how they should train, with the implication that if they follow his advice their "enjoyment" of alms and robes would be proper. He says :

> ... Monks, [you] should train in the following way : "Those donors of the requisites that we enjoy (*paribhuñjāma*)

> — namely, robes, alms-food, lodging, and medicine when ill — will have great fruit and benefit. Our renunciation will yield rewards; it will be fruitful; it will be of consequence." Monks, you should train in the above way. Monks, if you see your own benefit, you should strive with effort. If you see another's benefit, you should strive with effort. If you see benefit for both, you should strive with effort. (A.iv.124-35)

It is implicit in this passage that the earlier statements concerning a monk's enjoyment of requisites referred to improper ways. It is not enjoyment as such that is improper but the way things are enjoyed. Enjoying requisites merely for the sensual gratification they offer, a monk will be reborn in hell. Rather, he should reflect on the benefits that will accrue to the donors and on the benefits to be gained from the religious life. The "Blaze of Fire" discourse was so potent that it caused sixty monks to cough up blood, another sixty to leave the monkhood, and another sixty to become completely liberated (A.iv.135).

The commentary on the "Smaller Snap" states that after the "Blaze of Fire" Buddha did a half-month retreat, and when he came out, noticed a thinning of the ranks (AA.i.69). His cousin and aid, Ānanda, explained that many monks had left the order because they felt they could not fulfill the religious life; they felt that if they were practicing incorrectly, it would be improper for them to enjoy the food given to them by confident donors. Buddha expressed surprise that while he was in retreat, no one had explained to the monks the "causes for breathing easily" (*assāsakārana*), the sebeing practices by which monks are assured that they enjoy donations in the proper way.

In the "Smaller Snap" commentary, Buddha tells Ānanda that there are in his teaching as many causes for breathing easily as there are paths to the ocean (AA.i.70). He asks Ānanda to convene the monks and makes an introductory statement :

> Monks, just the rudimentary level of love (*mettāya sabbapubbabhāga*), merely relating to sentient beings with [the wish for their] welfare, [is a cause for breathing easily] — not just placement [love] or access [love] ! (AA.i.70)

The commentary adds that he taught the "Smaller Discourse on the Snap of the Fingers" to explain his point (AA.i.70). Thus, the "Smaller Snap," as a sequel to the "Blaze of Fire," was meant to indicate the ways in which the rudimentary level of love is a cause for breathing easily. It is noteworthy that according to this commentary Buddha establishes three levels of loving minds : the rudimentary level, which is merely the wish for sentient beings' welfare, and those developed at the levels of access and placement concentration.[1] In general, the compound "loving mind" can be interpreted as referring to any one of these three. In the "Smaller Snap" its meaning is restricted to the first.

In the "Smaller Snap" Gotama explains that if a monk sustains a loving mind for even the duration of a snap of the fingers he [deservedly] is called a monk. A "loving mind" is one "that relates to all sentient beings with [a wish for their] welfare" (AA.i.70). It has a universal scope, in so far as it wishes all beings to be happy. The commentary explains how a monk sustains such a mind :

> *Sustains.* How does he sustain [it] ? He sustains it while he thinks. He sustains it while knowing. He sustains it while seeing. He sustains it while reflecting. He sustains it while deciding confidently. He sustains it while applying energy. He sustains it while understanding with wisdom. He sustains it while directly knowing what is to be known by direct knowledge. He sustains it while abandoning what is to be abandoned. He sustains it while cultivating what is to be cultivated. He sustains it while realizing what is to be realized.
>
> Furthermore, it should be understood that he sustains it just by being devoted to relating [to sentient beings with a wish for their] welfare, which is the preliminary level of love (AA.i.70).

Thus, a monk can sustain a loving mind at any time in religious practice. He need only sustain a mind endowed with the preliminary level of love, for the duration of a fingers' snap, to [deservedly] be called a monk. He thereby fulfills the instructions, practices absorption profitably, and consumes (*bhuñjati*) the food of the kingdom unwastefully (A.i.10). He can breathe easily.

The commentary to the "Smaller Snap" cites the text as if it said "enjoys" (*paribhuñjati*, AA.i.70) instead of "consumes" (*bhuñjati*). "Enjoys" is a prominent word in the "Blaze of Fire" and, by the amended citation of this word from the "Smaller Snap," it emphasizes the relationship between the two discourses. The commentary explains how a monk who sustains a loving mind for even a snap of the fingers is "enjoying" the food of the kingdom without waste :

> *He enjoys* (*paribhuñjati*). There are four enjoyments : enjoyment of theft, enjoyment with debt, enjoyment of an inheritance, enjoyment as a master. With regard to this, when a monk endowed with wrong conduct enjoys [gifts], this is called "enjoyment of theft." When a monk endowed with correct conduct unreflectively enjoys [gifts], this is called "enjoyment with debt." When the seven groups of trainees enjoy [gifts], this is called "enjoyment of an inheritance." When a monk who has destroyed the harmful influences enjoys [gifts], this is called "enjoyment of a master."
>
> Concerning this, the monk [described in the "Smaller Snap"] enjoys the kingdom's food without waste for two reasons. [First] a monk who sustains love, even for just the duration of a snap of the fingers, enjoys the food of the kingdom as one who has become a master, as one who is free from debt, and as one who has become an heir. This is [one reason why] he enjoys the food of the kingdom without waste. [Second] the giving of a gift to a monk who sustains love, even for just the duration of a snap of the fingers, has great power. [He who gives a gift to such a monk derives] great fruit, great benefit, great splendor, and great effects [from his gift]. This is [another reason why] the monk enjoys the food of the kingdom without waste. (AA.i.72. Cf. Vism.i.125-28)

A monk who sustains, for just a short duration, a mind endowed with even the preliminary level of love has virtue comparable to that of a monk who is endowed with correct conduct, who reflects on the nature of donations, who is in one of the seven categories of trainees, or who has destroyed all the harmful influences — namely, a Worthy One. (The seven categories of trainees have experienced either the path or fruition-consciousness of the Stream-Enterer, the Once-Returner, or the Nonreturner, or the path-consciousness of the Worthy One.)

A patron who comes in contact with a monk who cultivates a loving mind becomes inspired by his carriage, demeanor, and conduct. This wholesome inspiration is the basis for pleasurable rewards in the future (P.P.xiv.nt.35) and can also serve as the seed for the patron's own subsequent religious practice. The practitioner who develops a loving mind is a fitting exemplar of the religious life, and he is thus consuming, or enjoying, his alms without waste.

The Loving Mind in Absorption

The term "loving mind" can refer specifically to a mind endowed with love at the level of absorption. For example, in the *Gradual Sayings*, Gotama teaches the householder Anāthapiṇḍaka a hierarchy of religious practices in terms of the results produced (A.iv.394-95) : almsgiving to a large number of people; providing nourishment for an individual endowed with right view (a Stream-Enterer) (AA.iv.185); for a Once-Returner; for a Nonreturner; for a Worthy One; for a nonenlightening Buddha; for a Perfectly Enlightened One; for the community of monks headed by Buddha; building a monastery; taking refuge in Buddha, in the Dharma, and in the Spiritual Community; observing the five precepts; cultivating a loving mind for an instant; and cultivating the perception of impermanence. The hierarchy of activities shows the relative importance of the cultivation of a loving mind; it is just below the cultivation of liberating insight.

The commentary explains the compound word "loving mind" : "*A loving mind* is a mind that relates to all sentient beings with [a wish for their] welfare. Furthermore, this is just included by way of placement [concentration]" (AA.iv.187). Thus, here a "loving mind" is endowed with all-encompassing love at the level of placement concentration/absorption (see below 42).

In the "Discourse on the Example of the Saw," Gotama teaches the monk Moliyaphagguna that he should cultivate a loving instead of angry mind (M.i.122-29). Moliyaphagguna had become so involved with the nuns that if anyone mentioned a fault in the nuns' behavior, he would become angry, and the nuns reacted similarly if anyone mentioned a fault in his behavior. Buddha hears about this situation and calls Moliya. He tells him that it is improper for renunciates to be too involved with nuns, that if someone should mention a fault in the nuns' behavior, he should maintain this attitude: "May my mind not become perverted. I will not utter evil speech. I will continue to have sympathy for [the others'] welfare. I will have a loving mind and be free from anger" (M.i.123). Buddha teaches Moliya that he should maintain the same attitude if someone should tell him his own faults or if someone should strike either him or the nuns.

Gotama instructs the monks to have a loving mind not only in the face of criticism but also when wishing to criticize others. In the *Dialogues of the Buddha* Gotama explains that if they wish to correct another monk they should do it at the proper time, speaking truthfully, gently, profitably, and with a loving mind (D.iii.237).[2] After advising the monks on how to speak to each other, he added that they should be gentle with one another (cf., above, pp. 12, 18).

In the *Middle-Length Sayings* Gotama teaches that anyone, regardless of caste, could cultivate a loving mind (M.ii.151). This practice is not only accessible to all and advisable in certain situations but also necessary for the completion of the spiritual path. In the "Lion's Roar to Kassapa" Gotama states that when a monk has cultivated a loving mind and destroyed all the harmful influences (*āsava*) he can [deservedly] be called a "wanderer" (*samaṇa*) or a Brahmin (*brāhmaṇa*, D.i.169). Here, Gotama is stating the religious criteria necessary for an individual to deservedly be called a wanderer or Brahmin in the ultimate sense (MA.ii.326).

The harmful influences (*āsava*) are listed in the discourses as desire, rebirth, ignorance, and wrong views.[3] These are interpreted in the commentaries as being synonymous with sense-desire, desire for rebirth, ignorance, and wrong views (Vism.xxii. 56). They are totally abandoned only by Worthy Ones, who have thoroughly seen the impermanent unsatisfying nature of worldly phenomena on a subtle level and have deeply tasted the satisfaction of the supramundane state, nirvāṇa. As a consequence, they are no longer attracted to the worldly pleasures of the senses or the transitory pleasures and pains of repeated rebirth. Such individuals have eliminated all mental obscuration and wrong ideas — a synonym for "Worthy One" being the compound word "one who has destroyed the harmful influences" (*khīṇasāva*). If such an individual, in addition, cultivates a loving mind, he can rightfully be called a wanderer or a Brahmin.

The Bodhisattva's Loving Mind

In the *Gradual Sayings* Buddha teaches the monks not to be afraid of meritorious activities, as these are actually synonymous with happiness (A.iv.88-91). He points to personal knowledge that meritorious activities which are performed for a long time lead to pleasing and enjoyable results, telling them that he himself, in a former life, had cultivated a loving mind for seven years (*mettacittaṃ bhāvetvā*)[4] and that he enjoyed a series of pleasing results. He was not reborn in this world for seven aeons of universal devolution and evolution; at the time of universal devolution he was born in the heavenly world of radiance (*Ābhassara*), and at the time of evolution he was reborn in the heavenly palace of Brahmā, where he reigned as the great god Mahābrahmā; he was Sakka, lord of the desire-realm deities, thirty-six times; he became a universal monarch and ruled righteously innumerable times. The loving mind that he cultivated and gave rise to these fruits is a mind conjoined with love at the level of one of the first three absorptions (AA.iv.44).

In another discourse the Bodhisattva's loving mind receives mention. In "On Fear and Terror" the Brahmin Jāṇussoṇi asks Gotama about the difficulties entailed in living in the forest (M.i.16). Buddha informs Jāṇussoṇi that those wanderers and Brahmins who live in the forest with angry or defiled minds would in fact evoke fear and terror in themselves (M.i.18). He explains to Jāṇussoṇi that when he himself was a Bodhisattva — a being training for Buddhahood — he lived in the forest, but had a loving, not an angry mind. Experiencing a loving mind, the Bodhisattva felt no hesitation, fear, or terror. The commentary adds : "*I did not have a mind filled with anger.* With regard to this, he also means, 'I had a loving mind, a mind [wishing for others'] welfare.' Bodhisattvas are like that" (MA.i.116). Since later in this discourse Gotama describes his enlightenment, it is reasonable to suspect that this discussion concerning the

Bodhisattva's life in the forest refers to the period immediately preceding Gotama's enlightenment.

Disciples' Loving Activities

In several discourses disciples are either described as having or admonished to cultivate loving physical, verbal, and mental activities. A disciple is motivated to develop these because he possesses a loving mind (DA.ii.584-85; iii.957), which, as was shown in the previous section, can be endowed with love at the preliminary or concentrated level (see above, p. 26). That the commentaries do not specify which of these motivates loving activities means that it could be either. These discussions also shed light on activities motivated by sympathy, which is defined as the preliminary level of love (DA.ii.456).

In the "Discourse on the Great Complete Liberation from Cyclic Existence," Ānanda weeps over the impending separation from his teacher, Gotama (D.ii.143), who reminds Ānanda that he has often taught that all pleasing things change and disappear. Buddha comforts Ānanda by praising his loving service :

> Ānanda, you have attended the Harmonious One for a long time with loving physical activities...loving verbal activities...loving mental activities, which were beneficial, happy, nondual, and measureless. (D.ii.144)

The commentary elaborates :

> *With loving physical activities*, with physical activities such as giving him gifts, washing his face, and so forth, which were initiated by a loving mind. *Beneficial*, done for the increase of benefit. *Happy*, the meaning is these were done with happiness and pleasure, not with grief or suffering. *Nondual*...some perform [loving physical activities, and so on] just in the presence of others, but not in their absence. Others perform them just in the absence of others, but not in their presence. He [Ānanda] performed [loving activities] without making a division in this way [and thus his loving physical activities were nondual].
>
> *Measureless*, without a measure. He means, "your [loving] physical activities were so abundant that even the world system is too narrow and the peak of existence too

> low [to contain them]." *With loving verbal activities*, with verbal activities such as announcing the time for washing his face, and so forth, initiated by a loving mind. Also, having heard some teaching and just saying, "Venerable One, you said that well" (*sādhu bhante*), is loving verbal activity. *With loving mental activity*, having taken care of his body at the proper time, he used to sit in an isolated spot and initiate mental activity in the following way, "May the teacher be free from illness, free from trouble. May he be happy." (DA.ii.584-85)

The discourses also record that monks practiced loving physical, verbal, and mental activities among themselves. In the "Smaller Discourse at Gosiṅga" Gotama visits the monks Anuruddha, Nandiya, and Kimbila, who are staying in a park at Gosiṅga (M.i.205-207). Buddha asks the monks if they are well, receiving sufficient alms-food, and getting along well with each other — like a "mixture of milk and water." They answer that they are well and they have sufficient alms-food. Led by Anuruddha, they individually tell Buddha that they are getting along well, like a "mixture of milk and water," stating that since they consider it a great gain to live with such fellow religious practitioners, they offer loving physical, verbal, and mental activities to each other, both in their presence and absence. Anuruddha describes his devotion to the others :

> The following occurred to me : "What if I gave up my own mind and were to put myself at these friends' service ? . . . Venerable One, our bodies are indeed different; however, our minds are definitely one." (M.i.206-207)

The commentary elaborates on Anuruddha's description of his loving physical, verbal, and mental activities :

> *Loving physical activities*, physical activities that exist because of a loving mind. *In the open as well as unbeknown* [*to the others*], in the presence of the others as well as in their absence. ...
>
> With regard to this, physical and verbal activities in the presence of the others are possible when an individual lives with others; the others are possible when living

separately. Mental activity is possible under all circumstances. [For instance] Anuruddha sees that one of the [two other] monks living with him leaves a bed or chair outside in disorder or [leaves] wooden or clay articles [outside in disorder]. He does not create contempt by thinking, "Who used this ?" Rather, he picks the things up and straightens them out as if he had left them in disorder himself, or he takes care of the situation that requires it. These are called loving physical activities in the presence of others.

[For instance] one of the monks goes away and leaves his bed, seat, or monks' requisites in disorder. Just as above he [Anuruddha] arranges these things or takes care of the situation which requires it. These are called loving physical activities in the absence of others.

When he [Anuruddha] is living together with the [two other] elders and engages them in sweet and pleasing conversation, this is called loving verbal activity in the presence of others. It is the same when he engages them in friendly or courteous conversation, religious talks, or chanting. It is the same when he asks them questions or answers their questions, and so forth. Furthermore, when the [two] elders go away and he relates their virtues by saying, "My dear friends, the Elders Nandiya and Kimbila are endowed with correct conduct in such and such a way. They maintain such and such practices," and so on, this is called loving verbal activity in the absence of others. Loving mental activity occurs when, in the presence of the others or in their absence, he reflects, "May my dear friends, the Elders Nandiya and Kimbila, be free from enmity and free from trouble. May they be happy."

Venerable One, our bodies are indeed different, for bodies are like flour or clay which has been powdered and cannot be made into one entity. *However, our minds are definitely one*; he means, "Our minds are just the same in the sense that we are close and not divided, in the sense that we do not quarrel but agree with one another." How did they each give up their own minds and put themselves at the others' service ? [For instance] one of them has a defective pot; one, dirty robes; one, some repair work. When in this situation the one who has the defective pot says, "Friends,

> my pot is defective : it should be baked," the others do not say, "My robes are dirty and need to be washed," or "I have repairs that need to be done." They enter the forest, collect wood, cut it, repair the pot, and bake it. Then the others wash their robes and do their repairs. The same [cooperation occurs] at the very first announcement [by one of the others], "Friends, my robes are dirty; they should be washed," or, "My hut has deteriorated; it should be repaired." (MA.ii.239-40)

Instructions to Practice Loving Activities

In the "Advice to Siṅgāla Discourse" Gotama teaches the householder Siṅgāla to attend to wanderers and Brahmins with loving physical, verbal and mental activities, by keeping his door open, and by providing them with material sustenance. The monks in turn will respond with activities motivated by sympathy. The commentary elaborates :

> *With loving physical activities.* In this and the following statement, the physical activities and so forth that are done once an individual has created a loving mind are called loving. [When a householder] goes to the monastery thinking, "I will consult the monks," takes hold of a pot with a strainer and strains some water, rubs the monks' feet or their backs, and so forth, these are called loving physical activities. [When a householder] sees the monks enter [the village] for the sake of alms-food and says, "Respectfully give them rice-milk, give them food," and so forth, this is called loving verbal activity. Also, [when he] respectfully and warmly listens to the dharma and says "You said that well," and so forth, these are called loving verbal activities. [When a householder] thinks, "May the elders who depend on our family be free from enmity and disturbance," this is called loving mental activity. (DA. iii.957)

In the "Discourse on the Great Complete Liberation from Cyclic Existence," Gotama teaches the monks that there are six conditions that will lead to gain (D.ii.80-81):[5] offering loving physical, verbal and mental activities to fellow practitioners both openly and unbeknown to others, sharing alms with fellow practitioners, being endowed with correct conduct, and possessing the view that will ultimately lead to the destruction of suffering. Buddha says that as long as they maintain these six conditions, they could expect to advance and not to fail. The commentary explains :

> *Loving physical activities* are physical activities done with a loving mind. The same holds true for [loving] verbal and mental activities. These are [prescribed] to monks in this text but householders may perform them as well. When monks, motivated by a loving mind, maintain proper conduct, this is called their loving physical activity. When householders go to a reliquary or to the Tree of Enlightenment for the sake of veneration, go to extend an invitation to the spiritual community, go to meet the monks when they see them enter the village for the sake of alms, take their alms-bowls, point out seats to them, or accompany them and so forth, these are called their loving physical activities. When the monks, motivated by a loving mind, teach the descriptions of correct conduct, explain the objects of meditation, or teach dharma, these are called their loving verbal activities. Also, [sustaining] the *Three Baskets* (*Tepiṭakam*), which contain the words of Buddha, [through question and explanation][6] is called their loving verbal activity. Householders' loving verbal activities occur when they say, "Let us go to the reliquary for the sake of veneration," "Let us go to the Tree of Enlightenment for the sake of veneration," "Let us create an opportunity for the dharma to be heard," "Let us offer homage with lamps, garlands, and flowers," "Let us maintain the three good practices [correct conduct, concentration, wisdom]," "Let us give out ticket-food, and so forth," "Let us make donations to a monk who is living in retreat during the rainy season," "Today, let us give the four requisites [robes, begging bowl, bed, and medicine] used by the spiritual community," "Extend an invitation to the spiritual community and prepare hard food, and so forth, for them," "Point out seats to them," "Provide them with water," "Go meet the monks and escort them back," "Have them

sit in their appointed places," "Serve them with zeal and energy," and so forth. When the monks rise early, attend to their bodies, go to the clearing near the reliquary and perform their customary activities, sit down at an isolated spot and think, "May the monks in this monastery be happy; may they be free from enmity and free from trouble," this is their loving mental activity. When the householders think, "May the noble ones be happy; may they be free from enmity and free from trouble," this is their loving mental activity.

Openly and unbeknown to others, in the presence of others and in their absence. [When monks] go to assist the novices in preparing their robes, this is called loving physical activity in the presence of others. Furthermore, all acts of homage such as washing the feet of the elders, greeting them respectfully, fanning them, and so forth are loving physical activities in the presence of others. If either [novices or elders] leave wooden articles or the like in disorder and a monk straightens them up without creating contempt, as if he had left them in disorder himself, this is called loving physical activity in the absence of others. Respectful words such as, "The Elder Deva, the Elder Tissa," constitute loving verbal activities in the presence of others. When [the Elder Deva and the Elder Tissa] are not in the monastery and a monk [using] possessive words asks, "Where is our Elder Deva, our Elder Tissa ? When will they come back ?" this is loving verbal activity in the absence of others. Looking warmly at others with fond, affectionate, loving eyes constitutes loving mental activity in the presence of others. Reflecting, "May the Elder Deva and the Elder Tissa be free from illness and free from discomfort," constitutes loving mental activity in the absence of others. (DA.ii.531-32)

This commentary states, "When the monks, motivated by a loving mind, maintain proper conduct, this is called their loving physical activity" (above, p. 55). This mixture of love and propriety is noteworthy. According to the Theravāda discourses and commentaries, a wholesome mind comprises a delicate mixture of diverse factors. A wholesome mind endowed with love would always be endowed with the mental factors of confidence, mindfulness, conscience, shame, nongreed, evenness, tranquillity, lightness, flexibility, efficiency, proficiency, and straightforwardness.[7]

As motivations for proper conduct, conscience and shame are said to be present in every wholesome state of mind. Conscience and shame do not connote neurotic guilt but rather factors stimulating behavior proper from one's own and others' point of view, respectively (Vism.xiv.142). Correct knowledge of propriety, far from implying neurotic guilt or self-hatred, depends upon their absence. (See, for example, S.iv.317-21). When an individual engages in self-hatred or feels fraught with guilt, he has no conscience or shame (Vism.xiv.92,170), for at such a time he is not doing what is proper or beneficial to himself or others. Since proper moral conduct is motivated by knowledge of propriety free from self-hatred, inflexibility, or guilt, ethical knowledge and conduct are possible without emotional strain. Through training one learns how to maintain correct conduct in a context of mental balance, flexibility, and lightness, abandoning unwholesome attitudes, such as self-aversion, that might arise and motivate behavior. If one errs in conduct, the remedy is in the recognition of error and the intention to reform and not in neurotic remorse.

In this context, conscience and shame are not discordant with other wholesome mental factors, including love, which can coexist with correct conduct without the slightest resentment, guilt, or inflexibility. Love, conscience, and shame are accompanied by the feeling of either mental pleasure or equanimity (Vism.xiv.83), and thus righteousness can occur with love and joy.

Beneficiaries of Loving Activities

In the discourses loving activities, as a group, are discussed only in terms of being extended to religious practitioners. There are the descriptions of Ānanda's to the Buddha and the monks Anuruddha, Kimbila, and Nandiya's to one another; there are Gotama's exhortations to the monks to practice loving activities toward one another because such lead to their advancement and his exhortation to Siṅgāla to take care of wanderers and Brahmins with loving activities because wanderers and Brahmins would then sympathize with him in return. The primary recipients of the loving activities discussed in the discourses are the monks. It must also be understood, however, that the populace at large would benefit from the monks' correct conduct and their teaching.

The exhortations concerning loving activities toward monks left much room for abuse, as they might be tempted to demand loving activities from laypersons. This explains the rigor with which Gotama taught about the proper way for monks to "enjoy" their alms. Those who receive loving activities obviously benefit, but those who perform them also experience immediate benefit. Since loving physical, verbal, and mental activities are initiated by a wholesome loving mind, the practitioner performing these activities would immediately experience the benefits associated with this state of mind.[8]

Chapter Four

LOVE

Acts of Love Toward the Teacher

In the *Gradual Sayings* Buddha describes six praiseworthy results that inspire a monk to develop the perception of suffering with regard to all conditioned phenomena (A.iii.443).

1. the perception of nirvāṇa will become established among all conditioned phenomena,
2. the mind will turn away from all realms,
3. the monk will see the peace which is nirvāṇa,
4. inherent tendencies [to defilements and rebirth] will be destroyed,
5. the monk will have completed his tasks, and
6. the monk will have served the teacher with acts of love.

In other words, through the development of the perception of suffering with regard to all conditional phenomena the benefits of being a Worthy One will arise.

The commentary explains "acts of love" : "*With acts of love*, by service united with love. For the seven [categories of] trainees serve the Harmonious One with acts of love. He who has destroyed the harmful influences has [completely] served the teacher [with acts of love]" (AA. iii.415). Trainees, namely, individuals have experienced the paths and fruitions of a Stream-Enterer, Once-Returner, Nonreturner, and the path of a Worthy One — have not completely served the teacher with acts of love, but a fully liberated person, one who has attained the fruition stage of a Worthy One, has. Through thoroughly understanding the suffering of all conditioned phenomena, he has extirpated every trace of desire for repeated rebirth. He has understood the impermanence and insubstantiality of conditioned phenomena to such an extent that he no longer has defiled reactions of attachment or hatred toward them. He has destroyed all the harmful influences that previously existed in his mind and has fully comprehended the peace of nirvāṇa. He is said to have completely served the teacher with acts of love. Thus, here "acts of love" refer to the insights that forever liberate a person from mental defilement. In this discourse "love" has the metaphoric meaning of insight.

Similarly, the commentary to the "Smaller Snap" (see, p. 26) says that a monk sustains a loving mind when he directly knows what is to be known by direct knowledge. Though this makes love contemporary with profound insight — the realization of nirvāṇa — Dhammapāla in his commentary to *The Path of Purification* makes it clear that love in its usual sense *cannot* occur in this context (P.P.xiv.nt.67).

Those mental factors which relate to sentient beings — namely, love, compassion and so forth — do not occur when the meditator's mind has nirvāṇa as its object (P.P.xiv.nt.67). The *metaphoric* equation of love with insight in the discussion of the above passage from the *Gradual Sayings* suggests that this same usage is occuring in the commentary to the "Smaller Snap" making the latter commentary consonant with Dhammapāla's view.

Love and Anger

According to the commentaries, love can exist at three levels — rudimentary, access, and placement (above p. 26). Apart from the above metaphoric use of "love," however, every instance of "love" (*mettā*) in the discourses is associated implicitly or explicitly with the strength of either access or placement concentration.[1] This distinguishes the usage of "love" from that of "loving." The latter refers to a state of mind or an activity that possesses or reflects *any* strength of love, from the rudimentary level up to placement.

In the *Gradual Sayings* Gotama informs the monks that he sees no other phenomenon to compare with the "liberation of the mind which is love" (*mettā cetovimutti*) in its ability to prevent anger from arising and in its ability to remove anger that has already arisen (A.i.4).[2] Gotama tells the monks that if they would pay careful attention to liberating love, then either anger would not arise in them or if it did, they would be able to remove it. The commentary explains why love is a liberation of the mind :

> *The liberation of the mind which is love.* It is love as it relates to all sentient beings with [the wish for their] welfare.

> Moreover, since the mind conjoined [with love] is liberated from all adverse factors such as the hindrances,[3] and so forth, it is called a liberation of the mind. Specifically, one should understand that because the mind is liberated from becoming possessed by anger, it [love] is a liberation of the mind.
>
> With regard to this, to the extent that it is love, even the preliminary aspect [of love] fits the case. Here, however, by saying "liberation of the mind," he meant just the placement [of love, as it were, into its object] by way of the first three . . . absorptions. (AA. i.47)

If an individual is instrumental in saving others from disaster, it is said that he is their "salvation"; the cause is given the name of the effect. Similarly, when love is systematically cultivated to absorption, it decisively and sustainedly liberates the mind from the hindrances. Since love has specific efficacy for liberating the mind from anger it receives the name of its effect, the "liberation of the mind."

The first absorption is free of the hindrances and possesses the five predominant factors of initial application of the mind to its object (*vitakka*), sustained application of the mind to its object (*vicāra*), pleasurable interest (*pīti*), bliss (*sukha*), and concentration (*samādhi*) (Vism.iv.107). What makes this state of mind unusual is the combination of deep concentration and bliss. Under normal circumstances, when an individual concentrates his mind, there is so much stress involved that bliss is impossible. The training to attain the first absorption involves learning how to balance the energy of effort with the serenity of concentration so that a sharp yet tension-free concentration of mind results. Such a state will be accompanied by the refreshing experience of bliss.

Buddhaghoṣa, in *The Path of Purification*, gives an evocative simile for the nature of the balanced effort necessary for proper concentration. Surgeons in India used to train by making incisions in lotus leaves floating on water (Vism.iv.68). Those students who were overanxious would either sink the leaf or cut it completely in two. Those who feared this consequence would not apply any pressure to the leaf and would fail to cut it at all. Those who succeeded had balanced energy and could make an incision without sinking the leaf or cutting it completely in two. The effort to achieve concentration must be balanced in a similar way, being neither too tense and heavy nor too light and dreamy. To achieve a balanced form of concentration takes training and care. Therefore, the experience of a state such as liberating love which is accompanied by bliss is rare.

During absorption the mental factor "initial application of mind" (*vitakka*) acts as if it were *evenly placing* the mind and its co-arisen mental factors *into* the object of absorption (P.P.iii. nt.4). This is the unique characteristic of this mental factor at this level of concentration. Attachment, on the contrary, *grasps at its* object (Vism.xiv.162). In addition, attachment is always accompanied by agitation, which is the tendency to be diffuse, or distracted.[4] Attachment involves perpetual frustration because its ever-present ally, agitation, prevents realization of its goal—satisfying union with its object.

The mental factor "initial application of mind" (*vitakka*) is also called "placement" (*appanā*) because of its ability to, as it were, place the mind into its objects (M.iii.73; P.P.iii.nt.4). However, because all absorption states of mind and their associated mental factors partake of this ability, they are all qualified by the epithet "placement" (P.P.iii.4). Thus, in the above commentary, "placement" refers to love at the level of absorption, which has this same ability.

The steps a meditator would take in cultivating the liberation of the mind, love, are fully discussed in *The Path of Purification* (chap. ix). In brief, the process involves universalizing and deepening the love already possessed. The beginner starts with himself and wishes, "May I be happy, may I be free from enmity." Then, realizing that just as he desires to be happy, so do others, he naturally experiences the wish for others' happiness and welfare. He then proceeds to cultivate love for one of his dear, pleasing, and revered religious teachers. It is said that a practitioner through remembering his teacher's inspiring and pleasing words or his admirable conduct and learning, is easily able to reach placement love with regard to him. The practitioner then proceeds to develop love in steps for a dear friend (not of the opposite sex, in the case of beginners), a neutral person, and a person with enmity toward him. This means that he makes his mind thoroughly flexible and efficient in generating love toward each of these individuals, in turn. Now, it is quite likely that the practitioner, upon calling to mind the person with enmity, will develop hostility himself. To counteract this, Buddhaghoṣa offers several different contemplations to displace hostility once it has arisen and diminish the likelihood of its recurrence in the future. Of these, two can be cited here.

The first is that individuals inherit the results of their deeds (Vism.ix.23-24). If the practitioner develops hostility, he can observe that at the same time he is experiencing the mental suffering associated with aversion (Vism.xiv.92). Furthermore, he is creating the causes and conditions for re-creating more hostility in the future, for attaining painful rebirths after death, and for failing to achieve any spiritual progress. If he abandons hostility, he will free himself from the mental suffering associated with aversion. Furthermore, he will be creating the causes and conditions for less hostility in the future, for attaining pleasurable rebirths, and for achieving spiritual progress. Also, since the individual with enmity toward the practitioner is harming himself in all the ways mentioned above, there is no need to seek personal vengeance against such a person. Through the operation of the laws of cause and effect, that person is reaping and will reap more pain than anyone would wish another.

The second is that there is no person who at some time has not been one's own mother, father, sister, or brother (Vism.ix.36). Because rebirth extends back infinitely, there is no person in the world today who has not been in a close relationship to us. As our mother, the individual for whom we now have hostility took care of us by carrying us in her womb, cleaning us — without objection — of every type of waste, and so on. As our father, this individual worked long, hard hours to support us. As our sister or brother, this individual helped us in various ways. Thus, it is not fitting to maintain hostility to this person, in the face of what they have done for us in the past.

Through regular attention to these contemplations, the practitioner will become ever more adept at displacing anger arising in the course of cultivating love toward a hostile individual. Having displaced this and achieved some mental balance, the practitioner can proceed to develop love toward this individual by taking the love he has felt for himself, his teacher, and the neutral person, and directing it toward this person. Thus, the practitioner must develop a strong experience of love with regard to these and then carry it over to the individual with enmity. In this practice the meditator is deliberately trying to affect his reactions to all beings with a wish for their welfare.

If the practitioner succeeds in developing a love that is in all ways even with regard to himself, a dear friend, a neutral person, and an enemy, he is said to have broken down the barriers between himself and others (Vism.ix.40-42).[5] This marks the attainment of access love. The practitioner then proceeds to deepen and concentrate this to the level of placement, wherein it is said to have penetrating force. The practitioner would then systematically increase the number of beings included in the range of his love, developing this attitude toward larger and larger groups at the level of absorption, till its range is universal.

In the *Kindred Sayings* the spirit Manibhadda utters a verse to Gotama :

> The mindful one is always fortunate.
> The mindful one finds happiness.
> For the mindful one, tomorrow is better.
> He is released from enmity. (S.i.208)

Gotama responds with verses :

> The mindful one is always fortunate.
> The mindful one finds happiness.
> For the mindful one, tomorrow is better.
> He is *not* released from enmity.
> He who delights in harmlessness
> The whole day and night
> And loves all beings
> Has no enmity for anyone. (S.i.208)

Gotama's verses indicate that one who practices mindfulness is not liberated from enmity, but that one who delights in harmlessness all the time and loves all beings is. The commentary asserts that no matter to what extent an individual has the thought "I am mindful," he will not be liberated from enmity (SA.i.305). It also clarifies that the individual referred to in Buddha's second verse is a Worthy One, who is said to cultivate love and compassion and to be free from enmity. What is the meaning of this commentary ?

According to *The Path of Purification*, mindfulness is a wholesome mental factor (Vism.xiv.133). It is implicit in the commentaries (and explicitly stated in at least one subcommentary) that wholesome mental factors cannot coexist with unwholesome mental factors.[6] When the wholesome mental factor mindfulness is temporarily present, no unwholesome ones can be present.[7] Thus, if a practitioner is mindful of a previous moment of anger, his mind in the present moment will necessarily be free from anger. Having a wholesome mind, he would be possessed of the thirteen mental factors that always coarise with it — confidence, mindfulness, conscience, shame, nonhate, nongreed, evenmindedness, tranquillity, lightness, flexibility, efficiency, proficiency, and straightforwardness (Vism.xiv.133). He would experience one of the two feelings that are associated with a wholesome mind — mental pleasure or equanimity (Vism.xiv.83). The practitioner who develops mindfulness in the present is also creating a tendency for similarly beneficial states in the future. For such an individual, "tomorrow is better." However, according to Gotama, the displacement of enmity through mindfulness is not enough; the mindful individual is not released from enmity.

In other contexts, love is called a "liberation of the mind" because, when it is developed at the level of absorption, it temporarily liberates the mind from anger (AA.i.47).[8] The practitioner who skillfully develops love to the level of absorption frees himself from anger and enjoys the feeling of bliss associated with absorption. Might the commentators explain Gotama's above-quoted verse to mean that love should be cultivated to absorption in order to properly liberate the mind from enmity ? This possibility can be rejected since just as mindfulness, which only temporarily frees the mind from enmity by means of displacement, is not a satisfactory liberation from enmity, so love, which temporarily frees the mind by means of suppression, would not be a satisfactory liberation from enmity.

The commentary takes a different approach. It explains that the individual referred to in the first verse still practices mindfulness with the thought, "I am mindful" (SA.i.305). He has not realized the insubstantial nature of the self. He has not realized that, in practicing mindfulness, one kind of conditioned phenomenon is observing other conditioned phenomena (Vism. xx.83). He has not understood that only momentary mental and physical constituents exist, with no enduring self to be found in any of them. Such a person cannot eliminate either wrong view, status consciousness, or desire (Vism.xx.83). He cannot become free from the enmity that arises because of the frustration of desire.

The practitioner mentioned in the second verse is explained to be a fully liberated Worthy One, who realizes the momentary and constituent nature of all conditioned phenomena. He understands that in the ultimate sense there is no substantial enduring "I" to be found anywhere in the constituents of the body or the mind. He is no longer ensnared by such thoughts as "I am" or "I am mindful" (see, for example, S.iii.126-32). A Worthy One has seen phenomena in such a way as to liberate himself forever from all mental defilements, including enmity (Vism.xxii.64-77, 122). He is able to develop love and compassion at all times. His liberation from enmity is complete.

In the "Discourse on the Example of the Saw" Gotama teaches about the necessity of having a loving mind in difficult situations (M.i.126-29). Buddha tells the monks that they may be addressed in any of five ways : at an appropriate or inappropriate time, truthfully or deceitfully, harshly or gently, profitably or unprofitably, and by those with loving minds or those full of anger. Gotama informs the monks that in whichever way they might be addressed, they should cultivate a loving mind. He explains their training :

> May our minds not become perverted. We will not utter evil speech. We will continue to have sympathy for [the other individual's] welfare. We will have loving minds and be free from anger. We will continue to relate to that individual [who had addressed us] with love in our minds. [Making the entire world] the object [of our minds endowed with love], we will continue to relate to the entire world with minds endowed with love — that are untroubled, free from enmity, vast, enlarged, and measureless. (M.i.127)

The monks should take whatever love they have for the individual who addresses them and go on to universalize it.

The commentary supplies word-by-word explanations :

> *Whole*, possessing all sentient beings. *World*, the world of sentient beings. *Vast*, it has many sentient beings as its object. *Enlarged*, by being of the enlarged planes of existence. *Measureless*, because it is well cultivated. *Free from enmity*, without anger. *Untroubled*, without suffering (MA.ii.100)

The mind endowed with love described here is enlarged because it belongs to the enlarged planes of existence, the form and formless realms (Vism.iv.74; xiii.12). When the mind is cultivated to absorption, it is said to change realms. It enters either the subtle form realm when it is cultivated to the level of the first four absorptions, or the even subtler formless realm if it is developed yet higher. The states of mind associated with these realms are "enlarged" because of their great ("large") ability to abandon decisively, though temporarily, the defilements and because of their abundant ("large") rewards (Exp. 58). Since love can only occur at the first three levels of absorption (Vism. xi.111), here "enlarged" refers to one of these.

In this piece, the mind endowed with love is also described as "measureless." Usually, concentration that is well cultivated and occurs at least at the level of the first absorption is called "measureless" (Vism.iii.20), and in the first absorption and higher, concentration receives this epithet because it is free of all the limitations of the desire realm, such as sense desire, and so forth (Exp.i.58-59). This epithet, which refers to concentration at the level of absorption, indicates that the mind endowed with love described here is at the level of absorption.

Thus, in this discourse Gotama is teaching the monks that they should cultivate love to the level of absorption, thereby enabling them to deal with any type of speech addressed to them. Implicitly, then, if they succeed in cultivating love in meditation to some extent their minds would be endowed with love and its attendant benefits outside of meditation (see, also Vism.xii.30). In the period following meditation they would have the balance associated with a wholesome mind and experience the feelings of either mental pleasure or equanimity. It would be hard to disturb them.

Gotama continues in the "Example of the Saw" with an illustration of the strength and durability of a mind endowed with love. He asks the monks whether someone could destroy the earth by digging into it, urinating on it, and so forth ? They answer by saying no, because the earth is deep and immeasurable (*appameyya*). Gotama then goes on to compare the strength of the loving mind to the invulnerability of the earth. He tells the monks that if any one should speak to them in any of the five ways, they should maintain loving minds and relate to the person with their mind endowed with love. The monks should proceed to train as follows :

> [Making the whole world of beings] the object of these [minds endowed with love], we will continue to relate to the whole world with minds that are like the earth — untroubled, free from enmity, vast, enlarged, and measureless. (M.i.127)

Just as someone with a spade and pail cannot destroy the great earth, so the five kinds of speech cannot adversely affect an individual possessed of a loving mind (MA.ii.100). As the earth withstands onslaught because it is deep and immesurable, so too the mind endowed with love.

Similarly, Gotama instructs the monks to cultivate love so that their minds resemble space which cannot be painted, the Ganges which cannot be burned, and well-kneaded cat-skin bags which cannot be made to squeak when rubbed with a piece of wool. If the monks follow this instruction, their minds will not be easily tainted, inflamed, or rubbed the wrong way.

The Power of Love

In the *Kindred Sayings*, Gotama teaches that just as families with many women and few men are easily assaulted, so a monk who has not cultivated the liberation of the mind which is love is easily assaulted by nonhuman spirits (S.ii.264). Conversely, just as it is difficult for families with many men and few women to be assaulted by robbers, so it is difficult for a monk who has cultivated the liberation of the mind which is love to be assaulted by nonhuman spirits. He then advises the monks to cultivate this attitude.

In the same vein in "The Discourse on Love," which appears in the fifth collection of discourses, (KP.8) Gotama teaches the monks how to meditate so as not to be frightened and disturbed by mischievous dieties (KP.232-35) :

> What should the person skilled in profitable practices do
> When he becomes aware of the peaceful state ?
>
> He should be capable, honest, straightforward,
> Receptive, flexible, humble,
> Content, easily supported,
> With few activities, with few possessions,
> With steady senses, wise,
> Considered in his action, and not mimicking householders.
> He should not practice any low [conduct] at all
> That would arouse the criticism of the wise.
>
> [He should cultivate these wishes:]
> "May all beings be at ease, secure;
> May they all be happy in heart.
> Whoever is a breathing being,
> Stable or unstable without exception,
> Long, or those who are large,
> Medium, short, subtle, gross.
> Visible or invisible,
> Distant or near,
> Beings or those yet to be born,
> May they all be happy in heart."
>
> One should not cheat another.
> One should not be proud with respect to anyone anywhere.
> One should not wish others harm
> Through anger or aversion.
>
> One should cultivate an unlimited mind
> Toward all beings
> The way a mother protects her only son
> With her life.
>
> He should cultivate an unlimited loving mind,
>   without obstruction, anger, or opposition
> To the whole world
> Above, below, and across.

Standing, walking, sitting, or reclining,
He should be resolute in this mindfulness,
As long as he is free from fatigue.
Here this is called the sublime attitude.

Without wrong view,
With correct conduct and vision,
Having removed attachment for desire's objects,
He is certain to come to no new womb. (KP.8-9)

The commentary states that when the monks who were taught this discourse followed its instructions and developed love, the deities who had been disturbing them became pleased, happy, cooperative, and helpful (KP.252). Love, thus, has the power of affecting spirits' attitudes. This is corroborated by the story of the monk Viśākha, who cultivated love and thus caused the nonhuman spirits living in the vicinity to live at peace with one another (Vism.ix.64-69). Even if non-human spirits did not become cooperative to monks cultivating love, they would not be able to upset them. In the *Kindred Sayings* Gotama states that if non-human spirits took it upon themselves to upset monks who have cultivated the liberation of the mind which is love, they would tire themselves out (S.ii.265).

Nevertheless, a practitioner does not seek to protect himself from upset, or disturbance by non-human spirits, with fear and cringing. Rather, abandoning fear, attachment, pride, and so forth (Vism.xiv.133, 143,145), he cultivates love as a liberation of the mind/sublime attitude (both synonyms for absorption love [AA.i.47; Vism.ix.44]). His mind is then stable, balanced, and blissful (Vism.ix.111) and is resistant to any form of mental upset.

It is said that such a practitioner is protected from physical assault as well (Vism.ix.71; xii.30-35). For example, the laywoman Sāmāvatī, who was Gotama's foremost disciple in the cultivation of love (A.i.26), was able to prevent harm to herself through it. When her husband became deceived about her loyalty and tried to raise his bow to kill her, she and her retinue related to the husband with love, and he could not complete his intended murder (Vism.xii.35). However, there are exceptions to such protection from physical harm; Sāmāvatī herself, the most skillful practitioner of love, eventually died in a fire as a result of previous harmful actions she had performed.[9]

Though there is no instance in the *discourses* where a practitioner's love is explicitly stated to affect another person's attitude beneficially, in *The Path of Purification* love is said to have this power. Before a practitioner actually undertakes meditation on any of the forty objects for concentration or undertakes the development of insight, he is instructed to develop love in the following way :

> A monk who has assumed a subject of meditation should first delimit the spiritual community of monks living within the parish. He should then cultivate love for them with the thought, "May they be happy and free from disturbance." Then [he should cultivate love] for the deities living in that parish, then for the leading individuals in the village upon which he relies for food, and then for the humans there and all the sentient beings among [them]. Through [his] love for the spiritual community of monks [in his parish], he generates a tender-mindedness among his companions, and they happily live together with him. Through [his] love for the deities living in the parish, they become tender-minded and protect him with a thorough-going and suitable protection. Through his love for the leading individuals in the village upon which he relies for food, they become tender and properly take care of his requisites in a careful and suitable way. Through his love for the humans there, they become clear minded and they do not despise him when he wanders about. Through his love for all sentient beings, [they let him] wander everywhere without obstruction. (Vism.iii.58)

Since any admixture of fear or attachment in the above practice would temporarily taint it with unwholesomeness, it is to be conjoined with balance, understanding, and confidence. A practitioner must cultivate love in this way before taking up *any other* subject of meditation and must maintain it as part of his general practice (Vism.iii.59) in order to establish a proper context for his undertaking. The meditation on love is the soil within which concentration and, or insight are cultivated. Even when full enlightenment is attained this soil of meditative concern for others is maintained (A.i.181-184).

The above passage from *The Path of Purification* is the only instance in the discourses or their commentaries where it is explicitly stated that meditative cultivation of love immediately and beneficially affects others' attitudes. This teaching reveals an extraordinary dimension to love cultivated in absorption : practitioners can help others, not only through teaching, receiving alms, and being exemplars of the religious life, but through their meditative development of love as well. Presumably, the same could be said of the cultivation of compassion and sympathetic joy.

In the *Gradual Sayings* Gotama explains that a certain monk had been fatally bitten by a snake because he had not related to the four families of snakes with a loving mind (*mettena-cittena,* A.ii.72-73). Gotama states that if the monk had related to the four families of snakes with a loving mind, he would not have been bitten. Thus, in order to protect themselves from snake bite practitioners should relate to the four families of snakes with loving minds, using the following reflection :

> I have love for the Virupakkas and love for the Erāpatas.
> I have love for the Chabyaputtas and [love] for the Kaṇhāgotamakas.
> I have love for those without any feet and love for those with two.
> I have love for those with four feet and love for those with many.
> May those without any feet not harm me, nor those with two.
> May those with four feet not harm me, nor those with many.
> May all sentient beings, all breathing beings, all living beings, all together see auspicious sights.
> May evil come to no one.
>
> Buddha is measureless, the dharma is measureless, the spiritual community is measureless. Serpents, snakes, scorpions, centipedes, spiders, lizards, and mice have a measure. I have spread protection. I have established a safeguard. May all living beings retreat. I praise the Fortunate One. I praise the seven Perfectly Enlightened Ones.[10] (A.ii.72-73)

When Gotama states that Buddha and so forth are measureless, it should be understood that he is talking about the virtues of the Buddha, the dharma, and the spiritual community (AA.iii.103). Serpents and so forth, on the other hand, have measured virtue (AA.iii.104). Gotama shows the monks that by these two wholesome activities — developing love and enunciating religious truths — they can protect themselves, evoking harmlessness and retreat from harmful creatures.

Moreover, in the *Kindred Sayings* Gotama teaches the monks that they can protect themselves by means of love (*mettatā*, S.v. 168-169) with the example of an acrobat and his apprentice who have two opposing opinions on how they should protect themselves and each other. The acrobat says that he would watch out for the apprentice and that the apprentice should watch out for him, whereby they would protect each other and complete their act safely. The apprentice, however, says that he would watch out for himself and that the acrobat should watch out for himself. Gotama explains that the performers used the apprentice's method successfully and concludes that they should do the same through sustaining the establishment of mindfulness. In other words, the monks would help themselves by their own development of mindfulness, which in turn, would be of indirect benefit to others. The monks would exemplify the rewards of the religious life with their calm and mindful demeanor, thereby inspiring others. Gotama then states :

> Monks, he who protects himself protects others. He who protects others protects himself.
>
> Monks, how does he who protects himself protect others ? By sustaining [meditation], cultivating it, and practicing it frequently. Monks, in this way he who protects himself protects others.
>
> Monks, how does he who protects others protect himself ? By patience, by harmlessness, by the condition of love, and by the condition of tender care. Monks, in this way, he who protects others protects himself. (S.v.169)

If a practitioner takes care of his own mind with regard to himself and others, then he will benefit both others and himself. The commentary makes this clear :

> *By sustaining*, by sustaining an object of meditation. *Monks, in this way he who protects himself protects others.* A monk who abandons delight in [worldly] activity but sustains and cultivates a basic object of meditation day and night attains the state of a Worthy One. Then, another individual sees him and thinks, "This monk is excellent. He has practiced correctly." Having developed this conviction with regard to the monk, he will reach a heaven. Thus, "he who protects himself protects others."
>
> *By patience* means by patience and tolerance. *By harmlessness* means by compassion along with the preliminary level of compassion. *By the condition of love* means by love along with the preliminary level of love. *By the condition of tender care* means by tender care and sympathetic joy along with the preliminary level of sympathetic joy. *He who protects others protects himself.* With regard to this, a monk, by day or night, proceeds to produce the first three ... absorptions with regard to these sublime attitudes [compassion, love, and sympathetic joy]. Using these absorptions as his basis, he develops insight by thoroughly understanding conditioned phenomena and attains the state of Worthy One. Thus, "he who protects others protects himself." (SA.iii.227)

A Worthy One is a model to others of the rewards obtainable from the religious life. An individual who sees a Worthy One becomes pleased, confident, and inspired by his deportment and behavior. At that time the individual has a wholesome mind and is creating causes and conditions for becoming a Worthy One himself in the future. Because of this confident, wholesome mind, the observer will at the least be reborn in a heaven after death. Thus, a practitioner who protects himself in his own practice and becomes a Worthy One also protects others.

Though a practitioner would beneficially and directly affect others through the cultivation of the sublime attitudes of love, compassion, and sympathetic joy (see above, p. 51), the discourses do not mention this point.[11] Rather, they emphasize that one who cultivates these attitudes protects his mind from anger, cruelty, and displeasure toward others respectively.[12] In the discourse cited above, Gotama states that a practitioner protects his mind with regard to his attitude toward others by means of patience, harmlessness, the condition of love, and the condition of tender care. The last three attitudes are interpreted to mean the sublime attitudes compassion, love, and sympathetic joy, meaning that they are understood as universal love, and so forth, at the level of absorption (A.iii.224-25; Vism.ix.45).[13] These sublime attitudes protect the practitioner from negative attitudes such as anger and can be used as the bases for insight (see below, p. 75), through which he can proceed to permanently abandon all mental defilement. He thereby liberates himself from rebirth with all its attendant sufferings and becomes a Worthy One. In this way, the practitioner who protects his own mind with regard to his attitude towards others ends up protecting himself.

This discourse emphasizes the exemplary role of practitioners and the importance of their own religious progress. Even though it does not include explicit instructions on social activity, it should be understood within the broad context of the instructions on sympathy which state that practitioners' heartfelt concern for others should actively be expressed, primarily through teaching. We may feel a compelling connection between social concern and consequent social activity — that every discussion of the former should entail a discussion of the latter — but Gotama did not feel so compelled. He did relate social activity to social concern in his instructions on sympathy, simple compassion, and loving activities and, especially in his teachings on sympathy, set the stage for the practitioner's concerned orientation to all others both in personal practice and helpful fraternal activity. However, as in this discourse being discussed, Gotama did not feel required to relate his meditative teachings on love and compassion to subsequent altruistic activity, as the latter was taught in other contexts. Nevertheless, it can be understood that such activity would naturally tend to follow from such meditations. In discussing cultivated love and compassion, Gotama presented the unique virtues of these states — virtues that are not, for the most part, discussed in connection with the general terms of "sympathy", "simple compassion," and "loving activities." These unique virtues are their protective aspect, personal and psychological benefits, benefits for the next life, and soteriological benefits.

Benefits of Love

In the *Gradual Sayings* Gotama teaches that there are eight benefits that an individual can gain from the liberation of the mind which is love when it is sustained, cultivated, practiced frequently, made into a habit, made strong, undertaken, increased, and made into a commitment (A.iv.150). "The individual sleeps well. He wakes well. He does not see horrible dreams. He is dear to humans. He is dear to nonhumans. The deities protect him. He is not affected by fire, poison or weapons. If he has no higher realization, then he ascends to the world of Brahma [after death]" (A.iv.150). The commentary elaborates :

> *He does not see horrible dreams.* Even when dreaming, he sees only auspicious dreams; he [sees himself] as if he were developing veneration at the reliquary, or offering homage [to the Buddha, the dharma, and the spiritual community]. He does not see horrible dreams in the way others do — seeing themselves as if they were surrounded by robbers, as if they were overrun by snakes, or as if they were falling into a chasm....
>
> *He is not affected by fire, poison, or weapons.* In this context some tell the story of the cow. A cow was standing giving milk to her calf. A hunter, playing with a spear in his hand, thought, "I will hit that [cow]." He threw the spear, which struck her body but bounced off like a palm leaf. This was not due to the [cow's] power of access [love], nor to the power of [her] placement [love]. It was due merely to the fact that she had a strong state of mind [wishing] for the welfare of the calf. Love has great power in this way. (AA.v.82-83).[14]

The above are general benefits of the liberation of the mind which is love, but it is never stated in the discourses or the commentaries that these benefits necessarily occur under all circumstances (see above, p. 50). Even Gotama, with his great capacity for love and sympathy, was not free of enemies such as his jealous cousin Devadatta.

The inverse proportion between the strength of different states of mind and the degree to which their benefits for others are articulated is noteworthy. Sympathy, not specifically associated with any strength of mind, is said to lead practitioners to teach others, to accept alms from them, and to exemplify the religious life for them. Loving activities, which are dependent on a loving mind of any strength, include a host of activities that are helpful to others. Though the liberation of the mind which is love is not discussed in terms of its beneficial effects on others, it was no doubt understood, and therefore unnecessary to articulate, that its cultivation would deepen one's sympathy and thus affect one's subsequent activities for others.

There is a direct relation between the strength of an attitude and the benefits and justifications explicitly expressed. Sympathy, a naturally acceptable attitude and motivation, is never justified by a present or future reward. A loving mind, even at the rudimentary level, justifies a monk's consumption of alms, his practice of absorption, and his title of "monk." Furthermore, monks' loving activities toward each other, based on a loving mind of any strength, will lead to the prosperity of the monastic community. The benefits and justifications associated with the liberation of the mind which is love are, however, the most diverse and plentiful, for the most attention had to be given to articulation of the uncommon benefits associated with this high level of mind. It is implicit that this strength of mind would also yield the benefits of the less concentrated attitudes.

After giving the benefits of love in the above-quoted discourse, Gotama goes on to praise the development of love :

> The fetters of one mindful, who cultivates measureless love, become diminished.
>
> He sees the destruction of the foundations [of cyclic existence].
>
> He who has love for even one breathing being thereby becomes wholesome.
>
> The noble one sympathizing with all breathing beings collects enormous merit.
>
> Sagelike kings conquer the earth, filled with sentient beings.
>
> And then go about sacrificing the Assamedha, Purisamedha, Sammāpasa, Vājapeyya, and Niraggala sacrifices;

They do not amass even one-sixteenth of a sixteenth of [the merit] that [an] individual amasses by having a well-cultivated loving mind.
They are like all the constellations of stars [compared] to the moon.
He who does not kill, nor cause others to kill,
He who does not rob, nor cause others to rob,
He who has love for all beings,
Has no enmity toward anyone. (A.iv.150-51)

The commentary to this discourse explains :

> *The fetters become diminished. He sees the destruction of the foundations* [*of cyclic existence*]. This means that he who has attained the state of a Worthy One has abandoned the ten fetters. This consists of the destruction of the foundations [of cyclic existence. This state is attained] by insight in proper sequence. [It, in turn] has love as its proximate cause.
>
> Or, *the fetters become diminished*, [meaning] aversion and also the fetters related to aversion become diminished. *He sees the destruction of the foundations* [*of cyclic existence*]. Because he is endowed with love, he sees the so-called destruction of just those foundations [of cyclic existence] which are defilements. (AA.iv.68)

In the discourses, the fetters (*saṃyojana*) are ten factors that bind an individual to cyclic existence : wrong view of individuality, doubt, attachment to rites and rituals, sense desire, anger, desire for the form realm, desire for the formless realm, status consciousness, distraction, and ignorance.[15] Since all these fetters are eliminated by a Worthy One, he has destroyed all the foundations (*upādhi*) of cyclic existence. There is nothing left that will cause his renewed birth, with all its attendant and repetitive sufferings.

The commentary alludes to two of the distinct ways of abandoning defilements discussed in the commentaries — the method of permanent abandonment by uprooting them through insight (*samucchedappahāna*) and the method of temporary abandonment by suppressing them through concentration (*vikkhambhanappahāna*).[16] The first explanation refers to a Worthy One who has developed insight with "measureless" love as its proximate cause. In brief, he would have developed concentration up to the level of absorption by means of meditating on love[17] and then emerged from absorption and used his highly sharpened mind to penetrate the specific and general characteristics of mind and body.[18] Ultimately finding every aspect of mind and body unstable, changing, and unreliable, his mind would naturally have sought and ultimately have found the condition that transcends all worldly change and instability — namely, nirvāṇa. As a consequence of this profound insight into the changing world and changeless nirvāṇa, the inclination to create ensnaring mental fetters such as sense desire and so forth would cease. The newfound understanding would no longer support unwholesome reactions which would be abandoned forever.

The second explanation interprets the individual mentioned in the discourse as being merely endowed with "measureless" love. Such a person is completely, but temporarily, free from all aspects of aversion. Here, "fetters related to aversion" refer to the unwholesome mental factors related to aversion — envy, hoarding, and worry (Vism.xiv.170). When Buddhaghoṣa says, "He sees the *so-called* destruction of just those foundations [of cyclic existence], which are defilements," he indicates that the temporary suppression of the defilements by concentrated love is being alluded to here. The practitioner's defilements can become manifest again after absorption. However, during the absorption of love, the meditator will experience a satisfying bliss accompanying the balanced suppression of his defilements. Through developing measureless love he benefits either through using this state of mind as a basis for liberating insight or through enjoying the satisfactions associated with this state of mind.

In the "Chapter of Elevens" in the *Gradual Sayings* Gotama lists eleven benefits to be gained by an individual who cultivates the liberation of the mind which is love. In addition to the eight given above, "He quickly concentrates [his] mind. His complexion is radiant. He dies unconfused" (A.v.342).[19] No doubt because of all these advantages, Gotama also taught that on lunar observance days (*uposatha*) the disciples of the noble ones were to develop a measureless mind endowed with love for all beings (A.iv.390).

CHAPTER FIVE

THE SUBLIME ATTITUDES

In Gotama's times it was believed that an individual who went to the "world of Brahman" (*Brahmaloka*) after death would achieve the status of Brahman and become immortal.[1] Gotama, however, denied that rebirth in the world of Brahmā would lead to immortality.[2] According to him, the only way to immortality is the path to nirvāṇa (M.i.68; MA.ii.178). In the "Discourse to Those Possessing the Threefold Knowledge" (D.i.235-53), two learned Brahmins, Vāseṭṭha and Bhāradvāja, express doubts with regard to the path for commuion with Brahmā. Having heard of Gotama's fame as a religious teacher, they decide to take their questions to him.

Gotama does not question the young Brahmins on their presuppositions concerning communion with Brahmā, which they probably understood to be synonymous with immortality. If Gotama had, they would have been pressed to defend their views and, therefore, might have become intractable with regard to his instructions. Rather, Buddha cultivated their pre-existing interest in communion with Brahmā and taught practices that he held were profitable and could lead to it. However, he himself held that communion with Brahmā after death was a worthwhile goal only for those who could not aspire to the complete cessation of suffering in the immortal nirvāṇa (S.v.410; M.i.73). From Gotama's course of action in the "Threefold Knowledge," it is clear that he ascertained that the two young Brahmins were not ready for this deeper aspiration and adjusted his instruction accordingly.[3]

Buddha explains to the young Brahmins that if they, wishing to achieve rebirth in communion with Brahmā, merely beseech, implore, and praise their deity, it will be futile. Rather, they should give up involvement [with women (DA.ii.404)], enmity, disturbance, as well as all other mental defilement, and wield power [over their minds (DA.ii.404)].

Gotama asserts that he knows the way to communion with Brahmā from his own experience. The practices that should be assumed to attain communion include renouncing the householder's life and becoming a monk, practicing correct conduct including harmlessness, guarding the doors of the senses, practicing mindfulness and discrimination, being content, and abandoning the five hindrances — sense desire, anger, sloth and torpor, agitation and worry, and doubt.[4] These five factors are hindrances to wholesome states in general but receive special mention in instructions on meditation, as they are especially obstructive to it and must, therefore, be abandoned (at least temporarily) for absorption to occur (Vism.iv.104).

The above practices, from abandoning the householder's life on down, constitute the preparation for concentration in general (D.i.63-73). About a practitioner who succeeds in even temporarily abandoning the hindrances, Gotama says : "He who sees that the five hindrances are abandoned within himself becomes joyous. In one who is joyous pleasurable interest arises. He who has a pleasurably interested mind experiences bodily calm. He who has a calm body experiences happiness. He who is happy becomes concentrated" (D.i.250). This passage exemplifies the teachings on the dependent origination of phenomena in the discourses. Buddha analytically shows the causal sequence that will give rise to concentration, a sequence that comprises a spiritual alchemy (see also, A.v.2-4).

The brevity of the above discussion does not suggest the degree of effort necessary for the accomplishment of concentration. The process seldom occurs quickly, for it is difficult to sustain, for even a short period, mental clarity that is not tainted by sense desire, anger, displeasure, or agitation. In other discourses, Gotama explains in detail the ways for removing the hindrances (for example, M.i.118-22); in still others, the steps before that, and so on. The discourses as a whole can be seen as the extensive explanation of the causal sequences necessary to achieve liberation from cyclic existence.

Having taught the preliminaries necessary for achieving the concentrated states of absorption in general, Gotama concludes his discourse to the young Brahmins with a unique set of practices particularly appropriate for the attainment of communion with Brahmā. Since Brahmā cultivates and sustains the attitudes of love, compassion, sympathetic joy and equanimity (M.i.370-71; AA.ii.204), the technique for achieving communion with Brahmā after death is to cultivate these attitudes during one's life. Gotama describes the method :

> He [a monk] continually relates to [the beings in] one direction [such as north] with a mind endowed with love, then likewise to [the beings in] the second, the third, and the fourth [direction]; and in the same way [to the beings] upward, downward, and across. He continually relates everywhere, equally, to the entire world [of beings], with a mind endowed with love — a mind that is untroubled, free from enmity, vast, enlarged, and measureless.
>
> Vāseṭṭha, a strong conch-shell blower can resound [a tone] to the four directions with just a little effort. Whatever is a measured activity does not remain on that occasion, does not become established on that occasion [see below, pp. 67-69]. Through the cultivated liberation of the mind which is love, the same is the case. Vāseṭṭha, this is a path to communion with the Brahmās.
>
> Furthermore, Vāseṭṭha, the monk continually relates to [the beings in] one direction with a mind endowed with compassion ... sympathetic joy ... equanimity; then likewise [the beings in] the second, the third, and the fourth [direction] and in the same way [to the beings] upward, downward, and across. He relates everywhere, equally, to the entire world [of beings], with a mind endowed with love — a mind that is untroubled, free from enmity, vast enlarged, and measureless.
>
> Vāseṭṭha, a strong conch-shell blower can resound [a tone] to the four directions with just a little effort. Whatever is a measured activity does not remain on that occasion, does not become established on that occasion. Through the cultivated liberation of the mind which is compassion ... sympathetic joy ... equanimity, the same is the case. Vāseṭṭha, this is a path to communion with the Brahmās. (D.i.250-51).

When love, and so forth, are cultivated according to the above set of instructions (hereafter referred to as the fourfold instructions), they are called "sublime attitudes" (A.iii.225).

Love, compassion, sympathetic joy, and equanimity are not

defined in the first four collections of discourses; however, the commentaries and *The Path of Purification* do supply definitions and explanations. Because of the distinctive characteristics of each sublime attitude, it can be understood that when one is present the others are absent. With respect to the nature of love, it "has the characteristic of devotion (*pavatti*) to the aspect of [others'] welfare" (Vism.ix.93). "It has the function of offering welfare" (Vism.ix.93). The meditative cultivation of love is particularly effective for counteracting anger (Vism.ix.108).

Compassion "has the characteristic of devotion to removing [others'] suffering" (Vism.ix.94). "It has the function of not enduring others' suffering" (Vism.ix.94). The meditative cultivation of compassion is particularly effective for counteracting harmfulness (Vism.ix.108).

Sympathetic joy "has the characteristic of rejoicing" (Vism. ix.95). "It has the function of being nonenvious" (Vism.ix.95). The meditative cultivation of sympathetic joy is particularly effective for counteracting displeasure (Vism.ix.108).

Equanimity "has the characteristic of devotion to the aspect of even-mindedness with regard to sentient beings" (Vism.ix.96). "It has the function of seeing beings equally" (Vism.ix.96). The meditative cultivation of equanimity is particularly effective for counteracting lust (*rāga*) (Vism.ix.108). The sublime attitude equanimity is distinct from the feeling equanimity; the former is neutsality with regard to sentient beings; the latter is the feeling of neither pleasure nor pain that accompanies various states of consciousness (Vism.iv.158, 162).[6]

The functions of these four attitudes are stated in terms of what they motivate in an individual. *The Ultimate Light* offers somewhat more evocative definitions and epitomes :

> *Love* is the state of desiring to offer happiness and welfare with the thought, "May all beings be happy," and so forth. *Compassion* is the state of desiring to remove suffering and misfortune, with the thought, "May they be liberated from these sufferings," and so forth. *Sympathetic joy* is the state of desiring the continuity of [others'] happiness and welfare, with the thought, "You beings are rejoicing; it is good that you are rejoicing; it is very good," and so forth. *Equanimity* is the state of observing [another's] suffering

or happiness and thinking, "These appear because of that individual's own past activities." (Pa.ii.128)

There is a tension between the characterizations and the epitomes. Love, for example, is characterized as devotion to the aspect of others' welfare, a state of desiring to offer happiness; this implies a commitment to action. Love is epitomized, however, by the wish, "May all beings be happy," which stops short of *necessary* commitment to action. The reason for this is perhaps that in the discourses the teachings on love and compassion involve the cultivation of these attitudes in meditation.[8] Therefore, the teachings entail only the cultivation of the *wish* that others be happy and free from suffering. Though Gotama never articulated a link between the meditation on love or compassion and subsequent activity on behalf of others, it can be assumed that the cultivation of these attitudes would affect the nature and scope of a meditator's manifest fraternal activity. A practitioner developing concentrated universal love or compassion would be deeply moved to help a wide range of individuals, without exception.

The active facets of love and compassion are portrayed in the instructions on loving activities, simple compassion, and sympathy which were discussed earlier.[9] These teachings are not at all limited to meditative contexts. Since Gotama had indicated the motivation for social activity in these instructions, he could relate the discourses on love and compassion to more contemplative aspects of the religious life.

It should be noted that the connotations of the terms "love" and so forth in the Pali discourses and commentaries are different from the normal English connotations of these words. "Love" is not used in the discourses with regard to sexual or conjugal relations. In one important discourse in which Gotama explains the proper reciprocal relations between husband and wife, he states that a husband should "attend" to his wife, and that she in turn would "sympathize" with him (D.iii.190).

In cultivating love as a sublime attitude, beginners are cautioned against trying to develop it toward members of the opposite sex, as love can too easily become lust (Vism.ix.4, 6). The practitioner must always be cautious to weed out any traces of attachment clinging, or bias that might affect his development of love

(Vism.ix.93). With care this is possible. The meditator expands the range of his love by progressively cultivating it first toward himself, then toward a respected teacher, a friend, a neutral person, and finally a hostile person (see above, pp. 42-44). He must then equalize, deepen, and extend this attitude — his goal being concentrated universal love, which does not discriminate between self and other (Vism.ix.40-48).

Similarly, compassion becomes mistaken if sadness arises (Vism.ix.94). Though it is often felt that it is only through becoming sorrowful ourselves that we are truly compassionate to others, this is not so. Compassion consists only of wishing that others be free from suffering. We do not help others by being overcome by their misery. Between heartlessness, on the one hand, and being thoroughly overwhelmed by others' difficulties, on the other, there lies the option of care without grief. The practitioner must be ever alert to remove any sadness that arises during cultivation of compassion. He starts with a person who is suffering intensely and wishes that that person be free from suffering. Then he cultivates it for a dear person, a neutral person, and a hostile person (Vism.ix.80). If difficulties arise with regard to the hostile person, then the antidotes mentioned above can be applied (see above, p. 43). In order to make compassion a sublime attitude, the practitioner must equalize, strengthen, and universalize it.

Sympathetic joy means to take joy in others' success. It becomes mistaken when merriment or giddiness are produced and one is carried away with others' success (Vism.ix.95). Insofar as balance is a necessary factor if there is to be a wholesome mind, any loss of balance through over-involvement in others' success tends to lead toward unwholesomeness and thus would be a deviation from correct practice. In cultivating sympathetic joy a person begins with regard to the past, present, or future success of a dear friend (Vism.ix.85). He then progresses to the success of a neutral person and a hostile person. In the subsequent steps he proceeds as in the cases of love and compassion.

Equanimity is complete evenness of mind in perceiving others' happiness or suffering. It is cultivated only at the level of the fourth absorption (Vism.ix.111). Meditators are motivated to cultivate equanimity because they see the disadvantages in the first three sublime attitudes, each of which can be cultivated in any of the first three absorptions (Vism.ix.111). The first three sublime attitudes are conjoined with concern for sentient beings' enjoyments in that they are the wish that beings be happy and so forth (Vism.ix.88). Such a wish is seen as a disadvantage compared to the peace associated with the sublime attitude equanimity which is free from such concern. Furthermore, the first three sublime attitudes are very close to approval and aversion (Vism. ix.88). Love must be guarded lest it change into attachment; compassion, lest it turn into aversion and sadness at others' condition;[10] sympathetic joy, lest it turn into giddiness. These dangers are seen as disadvantages compared tc the peacefulness of equanimity, which need not be guarded in this way. Finally, the first three sublime attitudes are associated with the feeling of bliss because they are the means of escaping from enmity, harmfulness, and displeasure, all of which are associated with grief (Vism.ix.88, 111).[11] The bliss that occurs in the first three absorptions is seen as gross compared to the *feeling* equanimity that occurs in conjunction with the *sublime attitude* equanimity in the fourth absorption.[12]

Equanimity becomes mistaken if it turns into mere unknowing equanimity (Vism.ix.96, and below, pp. 85-86). Properly cultivated, equanimity involves the realization that others are owners of their activities, and thus their future circumstances will reflect the ethical aspect of their current activities (Vism.ix.96). While virtue leads to welcome consequences, nonvirtue brings the opposite (Vism.ix.23-24). Others must ultimately take responsibility for their own fate; the practitioner, for his. Mindful of this, the meditator frees his mind from all unwholesome approval and aversion towards others' conduct and sustains wholesome impartiality at the level of the fourth absorption .

Before actually cultivating the sublime attitude equanimity, the practitioner would cultivate one of the other sublime attitudes to the level of the third absorption (Vism.ix.104).[13] He would emerge from the concentrated state and develop equanimity with regard to a naturally neutral person, a friend, and an enemy. In the subsequent steps he proceeds as with the earlier sublime attitudes (see p. 65). The only exception is that when he strives for absorption with this attitude, he must achieve the fourth absorption.

With this understanding of the nature of the sublime attitudes, we can go back and look at the above-quoted simile of the conch-shell blower (see p. 62). The commentary explains it as follows :

> *Vāseṭṭha, a strong conch-shell blower*, and so forth....A weak conch-shell blower cannot resound [a tone] to the four directions even though he is blowing into a conch; he does not spread the sound everywhere. On the other hand, a strong one spreads [the sound everywhere]. *Through the cultivated liberation of the mind which is love :* with regard to this, when *love* is said, then either access [love] or placement [love] fits the case. However, when *liberation of the mind* is said, just placement [love] fits the case. *Whatever is a measured activity* : that [activity] which is in the desire realm is called a measured activity. That activity which is in the form and formless realm is called measureless activity.[14] It is called a measureless [activity] because it has transcended measured [activity] and because it has become expanded through relating to the directions specifically and generally. *Does not remain on that occasion, does not become established on that occasion* : That desire realm activity does not linger in the form or formless realm activity. It does not become established there. What does this mean ? The desire realm activity cannot find a footing in the form or formless realm activity and take its own opportunity to become established. It is only the form or formless realm activity that suffuses and overpowers desire realm activity and takes its own opportunity to become established. It is like the great ocean, which suffuses and overpowers the small pool, takes its own opportunity, and becomes established. It [the form or formless realm activity] pushes aside the ripening [of the desire realm activity] and just itself leads to communion with Brahmā. (DA.ii.405-406)

The commentary states that "love" can mean either access or placement love — love at the level of concentration just below absorption or at the level of absorption. Though this accords with the actual usage of "love" in the discourses,[15] as a liberation of the mind just placement love is meant. The same qualification applies to compassion and sympathetic joy. It also applies to equanimity, but only to equanimity in the sense of even-mindedness with regard to sentient beings.[16]

Just as a strong conch-shell blower, with little effort, can resound a tone to the four directions, so a practitioner, by means of the cultivated liberations of the mind, can relate to the beings in all the directions. When the strong conch-shell blower resounds a tone to the four directions, then no measured — that is, limited — activity remains or becomes established on that occasion. In other words, there is no place where the sound is not heard. The situation is said to be similar in the case of the liberations of the mind love, and so forth, but what does this mean?

First of all, with regard to states of mind, it is important to remember that the term "activity" (Pali : *kamma*/ English : *karma*) refers to "intention" (*cetanā*) (Vism.xix.14). By substituting "intention" for "activity" the commentary's position is clarified. Desire realm intentions are measured, like the limited suffusion of the weak conch-shell blower. When an individual achieves absorption, his mind is said to change realms, being no longer of the desire realm which is grosser than the form and formless realms. It is, then, either in the form realm, associated with the first four absorptions, or in the even subtler formless realm, associated with higher states of concentration. Since the states of mind associated with the sublime attitudes are among the first four absorptions, they are of the form realm,[17] and the intentions associated with these form realm states of mind are completely free of all such attitudes as lust, which restrict the mind and create a measure in or limit it (Exp.i.58-59). The intentions themselves are said to be measureless. Furthermore, a practitioner who cultivates the sublime attitudes expands them either by specific increment — gradually including beings in each direction, or by general inclusion — simultaneously, in one step, relating to all beings everywhere (Vism.ix.45-47). Thus, a meditator's intentions are measureless from the viewpoint of their realm and their objects. At the time when measureless intentions of love are present, no measured desire realm intentions can occur.

The commentary, using the images of the ocean and a pond, goes on to point out yet another meaning to the statement,

"Whatever is a measured activity does not remain on that occasion" (see above, p. 67). If an individual has cultivated one of the sublime attitudes at some point in his life, then, at his death, the intention associated with this attitude will come to fulfilment and lead to his rebirth in the world of Brahmā. It will not be possible for any measured desire realm activity to come to fulfilment at that time. The efficacy of the sublime attitudes in leading to rebirth in communion with Brahmā is thus guaranteed. The explanation extends the temporal scope of the simile of the strong conch-shell blower to include the results of cultivating the liberations of the mind — love, and so forth, at the level of absorption.

Gotama concludes the discourse by stating that one who would cultivate the four sublime attitudes in the above way would be free from involvement [with women], enmity, disturbance, and mental defilement, thereby wielding power [over his mind]. Such a person with Brahmā-like virtues attains communion with Brahmā after death.

Order of Development

When love, compassion, sympathetic joy, and equanimity are cultivated according to the method of the fourfold instructions they are called the "sublime attitudes" (*brahma-vihāra*, A.iii.225). Literally, the "sublime attitudes" are "ways of living (*vihāra*) like Brahmā [deities]" (*Brahmā*), or they are "the best (*brahma*) ways of living" (*vihāra*) (Vism.ix.106). Each sublime attitude is an antidote to an unwholesome reaction, such as anger, harmfulness, and so forth (see above, p. 63). Thus, all four are appropriate for every practitioner though a particular meditator might find one more useful at a given time and emphasize it.[18] Gotama emphasized the over-all benefits of the cultivated attitude of love, perhaps because of its relatedness to his teachings on loving activities and sympathy. An increase in love would vivify the latter two thus enriching the motivation and expression of the *whole* religious life.

The hierarchy of the sublime attitudes, with the first three on an equal footing and equanimity as the highest, reflects the psychological benefits of equanimity. In one commentary their order of development is compared to the attitudes parents feel for their children :

> ...When a youth is in the womb, the parents think with a loving mind, "When will we see our son healthy and endowed with all his major and minor limbs?" Then, when this tender creature lies on his back and cries or wails because of being bitten by lice or fleas or because of being bothered by troubled sleep, the parents hear this noise and feel simple compassion. Furthermore, when the parents observe the youth in his most desirable years, either at the time of his play while he runs and races or at the time he rests, their minds become tender, like a hundred fluffy balls of cotton soaked in the finest clarified butter. The parents' minds are satisfied and joyous. They have sympathetic joy at that time. Then, when the son is able to provide adornments for his wife and settle in his own house, the parents become even-minded and think, "Now our son can live on his own." In this way, they have equanimity at that time. (AA.ii.204)

In a similar way, the practitioner cultivating the sublime attitudes first develops love, wishing for the welfare of sentient beings (Vism.ix.109). Then when he sees, hears, or reflects that those beings are subject to suffering (Vism.ix.109), he cultivates compassion which is devotion to removing others' suffering. (Because this devotion is cultivated in a meditative state, the practitioner is concentrating on developing an attitude rather than an activity). When the practitioner "sees" (*disvā*) the prosperity of these beings whose welfare he wished for in his cultivation of love and whose suffering he wished removed in that of compassion, he rejoices (Vism.ix.109). Here, "sees" means the meditator either considers others' prosperity in the present or imagines it in the past or the future (Vism.ix.85), not limiting himself to the actual external situation that obtains at the time of meditation. Cultivating sympathetic joy in this way, the practitioner completes formation of concerned attitudes for others. Nothing remains to be done in terms of these attitudes, and thus he can cultivate equanimity, which is a devotion to evenmindedness. He observes beings as a neutral observer (Vism.ix.109).

A practitioner is motivated to develop any one of the sublime attitudes for their personal and psychological benefits[19] and to develop all four as antidotes to anger and so forth (see above,

p. 63). The prescribed order of development follows the pattern of four parental responses. Repeating this pattern over and over, the practitioner deepens his concern for others, as well as his ability to complement that concern with even-mindedness. It is implicit that cultivating these attitudes in meditation beneficially affects the intensity, appropriateness, and stability of manifest responses to the actual condition of others.

Faults of the Sublime Attitudes

Gotama never claimed that the fourfold instructions for cultivating the sublime attitudes were uniquely his.[20] He taught these meditations in the broad framework of the quest for liberation from mental defilement and rebirth. Anyone who made just the sublime attitudes their ultimate practice would be mistaken. Gotama clearly contrasts the mere practice of the sublime attitudes with his teaching of the eightfold path to liberation :

> ...that practice [namely, the mere cultivation of love, and so forth, according to the fourfold instructions] is conducive not to turning away, nor to dispassion, nor to quieting, nor to cessation, nor to direct knowledge, nor to enlightenment, nor to nirvāṇa, but only to rebirth in the world of Brahmā.
>
> ...my practice is conducive to complete turning away, dispassion, cessation, quieting, direct knowledge, enlightenment, and nirvāṇa — specifically the eightfold noble path, ...(D.ii.251)

The commentary explains :

> *Not to turning away* : it is not for the purpose of turning away from cyclic existence. *Nor to dispassion* : it is not for the purpose of [creating] dispassion with regard to cyclic existence. *Nor to cessation* : it is not for the sake of the cessation of cyclic existence. *Nor to quieting* : it is not for the quieting of cyclic existence. *Nor to direct knowledge* : it is not for the purpose of direct knowledge concerning cyclic existence. *Nor to enlightenment* : it is not for the purpose of awakening from cyclic existence by leaving the sleep of the defilements. *Nor to nirvāṇa* : it is not for the purpose of the immortal nirvāṇa.

> *To complete turning away* : it is for the purpose of just completely turning away from cyclic existence. With regard to this, *turning away* means insight; *dispassion* means the path; *cessation*, *quieting* mean nirvāṇa; *direct knowledge*, *enlightenment* mean the path; *nirvāṇa* means just nirvāṇa. Thus, at one place insight is mentioned; at three, the path, and at three, nirvāṇa. The systematic explanation should be understood in this way. Figuratively, however, all of these are synonyms for the path as well as for nirvāṇa. (DA.ii.670-71)

Mere cultivation of the sublime attitudes will lead to rebirth in the world of Brahmā and will not, alone, cause the permanent abandonment of defilements or freedom from rebirth. For even Brahmā deities are subject to aging, death, and renewed birth with all its attendant sufferings (A.iv.104). It is only through cultivation of Buddha's path which induces realization of nirvāṇa that one can ultimately achieve freedom from rebirth, change, and suffering in the peace of nirvāṇa (A.iv.104).[21] However, not all individuals were capable of assimilating Gotama's instructions on suffering and escape from it. Those who were not were taught other topics such as the cultivation of the sublime attitudes, which are helpful but not of the highest import (for an example see above p. 60).

Once, Sāriputta taught the Brahmin Dhānañjāni to cultivate the sublime attitudes in order to be reborn in the world of Brahmā (M.ii.195-96). Immediately following, Dhānañjāni cultivates the attitudes and dies, being reborn in the world of Brahmā. Gotama knows of these events clairvoyantly, and when Sāriputta returns, Buddha asks him, "Sāriputta, did you get up and leave once you established the Brahmin Dhānañjāni in the inferior world of Brahmā when there was something more to be done ?" (M.ii. 195-96) Sāriputta explains that he established the Brahmin in the world of Brahmā because Brahmins were committed to that world.

Buddha's question indicates that a teacher of religious practice cannot rest content with accommodating his student's interest. The teacher also has to press a student to the full extent of his capacity at any given time. Since achieving rebirth in the world of Brahmā is inferior to gaining insight,[22] if a student is ready for the latter, then it is the teacher's prime responsibility to transmit these teachings.

When individuals who possess profound insight cultivate the sublime attitudes, the faults described above are not entailed, for these are then being cultivated in a proper context.[23] Gotama stated that there is a distinct difference between the cultivation of the sublime attitudes by a worldling and by a knowledgeable disciple of the noble ones (A.ii.128-29).[24] When a worldling cultivates the sublime attitudes, he is reborn in the Brahmā worlds after his death, but after the expiration of his lifetime there, he is reborn as a hell being, hungry ghost, or animal (A.ii.129). Aside from Worthy Ones, who are completely free from all rebirth, any "knowledgeable disciple of the noble ones" who cultivates the sublime attitudes will also be reborn in the world of Brahmā after death (A.ii.129), but continue to practice there and become a Worthy One. When that life is finished, they are no longer reborn but gain the security of immortal nirvāṇa.

Gotama's Love, Compassion, Sympathetic Joy, and Equanimity

Even after his enlightenment Gotama continued to cultivate all four sublime attitudes according to the method of the fourfold instructions (A.i.183). His skill in all four attitudes was obvious to others; in one discourse, the householder Jīvaka Komārabhacca says, "Venerable One, I have heard, 'Brahmā lives with love.' That [Brahmā] is the Fortunate One [Buddha], I see clearly. For, Venerable One, the Fortunate One lives with love" (M.i.369-70). Since it was held that the Brahmā deities cultivated love, compassion, sympathetic joy, and equanimity (see also, AA.ii.204), Jīvaka identifies Gotama as a Brahmā because he sees that he lives with love. Gotama replies, "Jīvaka, that lust, hate, and delusion by which the Harmonious One might become angry is abandoned, cut off at the root, made into the likes of a baseless palm tree, destroyed. They will not be able to arise in the future. Jīvaka, if what you say is in connection with this, I accept it" (M.i.370). Jīvaka and Gotama go on to have the same interchange with regard to compassion, sympathetic joy, and equanimity. Gotama informs Jīvaka that whatever lust, hate, and delusion might have led him to become, in turn, harmful (*vihesāvant*), displeased (*arativant*), or filled with aversion (*paṭighavant*) had been destroyed. Buddha thus emphasizes to Jīvaka that his love and so forth arise in dependence on his abandonment of lust, hate, and delusion. In this discourse, Gotama establishes anger, harmfulness, displeasure, and aversion as the opposites of love, and so forth.[25]

The commentary explains Gotama's remarks :

> *Jīvaka, if what you say is in connection with this* : Jīvaka, Great Brahmā abandons anger and so forth by means of suppressive abandonment. He lives with love by that means. I [abandon them] by means of eliminative abandonment. *If what you say is in connection with this*: the meaning is, "If it is as above, then *I accept* your statement." He [Jīvaka] was receptive [to this]. Then the Fortunate One expanded the above teaching to him by way of the remaining sublime attitudes...(MA.iii.50)

Brahmā abandons the obstacles to love, and so forth, by suppressing them.[26] Gotama at the time of his enlightenment, however, had uprooted all mental defilement. Thus, when he cultivated love and so forth, he had to make no effort to suppress defilement. They had been totally removed through the cultivation of insight.

Insight and the Sublime Attitudes

To develop insight one first cultivates correct conduct and concentration. Correct conduct is the ever-necessary basis that allows one to be free from remorse for bad conduct (Vism.iv.23). Correct conduct sustains wholesome states of mind in the present and creates the conditions for similar states in the future (Vism. xiv.35). It is only within this causal framework of wholesomeness that one can hope to establish those refined states of mind associated with concentration.

Among the forty subjects suitable for concentration (Vism. iii.104), meditators choose one or more depending on their teacher's advice (Vism.iii.129). Then the meditator uses his mind sharpened with concentration as an instrument to penetrate the subtle nature of mind and matter. He cultivates insight.

If a practitioner has insight and, in addition, cultivates the concentrated states of the sublime attitudes, he is skilled in both as distinct aspects of practice (see above, p. 73). It is possible, however, to join these two types into one practice. In the "Discourse at the City of Atthaka" the householder Dasama asks Ānanda whether there is one practice taught by the Buddha that can liberate the mind, destroy the harmful influences (see above, pp. 29-30), and yield the unsurpassable freedom from bondage (M.i.349).

Ānanda answers by giving eleven practices that would accomplish this goal, one of which is :

> ...A Monk continually relates to [the beings in] one direction with a mind endowed with love; then likewise, [the beings in] the second, the third, and the fourth [direction]; and in the same way [to the beings] upward, downward, and across. He continually relates everywhere; equally, to the entire world [of beings], with a mind endowed with love — a mind that is untroubled, free from enmity, vast, enlarged, and measureless. He then reflects in this way: "Even this liberation of the mind which is love is produced and intended. Whatever is produced and intended is impermanent, is subject to cessation." He understands this. He becomes established in this [understanding] and destroys the harmful influences. If he does not destroy the harmful influences, then...he destroys the five lower fetters [see above, p. 58] and comes to have spontaneous rebirth [in a heaven]....(M.i.351).[27]

In order to cultivate insight according to the above method, a meditator first cultivates one of the sublime attitudes in the usual way. He then emerges from this concentrated state, but the clarity of mind in absorption carries over for some time subsequent to the actual absorption state (Vism.xxii.111). He gives up sustaining the sublime attitude and uses his now-sharpened mind to detect the nature of material and mental realities.[28] He distinguishes the different functions of the mental factors and the constituent nature of the material phenomena making up the body. For example, an attitude of love involves placing and sustaining the mind on beings. This accomplished, pleasurable interest arises. Without insight, these three coexistent mental activities — placing, sustaining, and being pleasurably interested — would be experienced as an undifferentiated indivisible state of mind.[29] With insight, they can be seen as three distinct mental processes with separate functions (Vism.xviii.3). This type of investigation is repeated in many contexts and in relation to different types of mental activities (Vism.xxi.112). Similarly, the unitary mass of materiality can be experientially perceived to be made up of discrete constituents. Instead of concepts such as "being", "arm", "head", and so forth, the meditator attends to his bare physical experiences. Therein, he notices areas of hardness or softness, heat or cold, and so forth. What was formerly conceived as a compact mass[30] is now seen to be made up of discontinuous physical experiences.

As the individual material and mental constituents of personality become clear their common characteristics become manifest (Vism.xx.3). Each of the discrete mental and material components is seen to be changing, unstable, and with no substantial continuity from one moment to the next; thus, they are all unsatisfactory. The meditator begins to cognize directly the quanta of experience that are the building blocks of every day perceptions. Since even the cognizing consciousness is subject to dissolution, it becomes clear that one moment of consciousness totally ceases and is then followed by another moment of consciousness (Vism.xxi.13). Not finding a refuge, a permanent self, in the changing pithless elements of his personality or his environment, the meditator sees all conditioned phenomena "as impermanent, as suffering, as illness, as boils, as arrows, as grief, as affliction, as alien, as dissolving, as empty, and as selfless" (A.ii.130). Within this new perception of the nature of reality, the yogi quite naturally seeks an escape. He finds it in the realization of nirvāṇa, experiencing a brief cognition of a condition that is beyond all instability and change.

Earlier, in the preliminary stages of insight, his view of the conditioned world was considerably altered through the sharp perceptions of unsatisfactoriness afforded by a concentrated mind. Then, with the realization of nirvāṇa he becomes aware of what true peace is. Having experienced ultimate quiet, he will no longer relate to even the most alluring mundane attractions in the same way. The unreliability and transience of all conditioned phenomena is clear, as is the security of nirvāṇa.

The meditator must continue to sharpen his mind with concentration and to develop insight after becoming a Stream-Enterer, passing through three stages of ever-deepening realization.

In these, the unsatisfactory nature of conditioned phenomena becomes clearer and clearer. Similarly, the totally unsullied nature of nirvāṇa becomes ever more distinct. With the fruition of the Worthy One, insight is complete. Freed from rebirth, at death he attains the immortal state of nirvāṇa.

In this way, the sublime attitudes are used as a basis for ultimate liberation from cyclic existence. With even the realization of a Stream-Enterer, a practitioner becomes capable of teaching others the path of insight.

Chapter Six

EQUANIMITY

One of the most common technical terms in the Theravāda discourses is "equanimity" (*upekkhā*). The term often refers to neutral feelings but also has several other uses in the sense of even-mindedness — an ethical goal. Because of this latter usage, equanimity has drawn the interest of modern scholars; two of the most widely quoted Western writers on South Asian Buddhism, Winston King and Melford Spiro, pay particular attention to it in their characterization of Theravāda.[1]

Both King and Spiro have bifurcated Theravāda Buddhism, finding one part of the religion devoted to the means for attaining pleasurable rebirth, the other to escape from rebirth altogether. The former has to do with wholesome intentions and activities (*kamma*) which insure rebirth as a human or in heaven; they have termed this "kammatic Buddhism" and the other "nibbanic Buddhism."[2] At the time that nirvāṇa is realized, one of the predominant conditioning mental factors (*saṅkhāra*) is equanimity (to be discussed below), and thus King also calls "nibbanic Buddhism," the "Ethic of Equanimity."[3] King holds that this ethic is the basis of monastic Buddhism and that it entails "withdrawal from the active life of historical involvement into the life of intense contemplation; it is the search for an experience of the timeless and ultimate."[4] The core of this ethic, according to King, is the sublime attitude equanimity (*brahmavihāra-upekkhā*) which he identifies as the equanimity which occurs when nirvāṇa is realized (*bojjhaṅga-upekkhā*).[5]

Spiro, in parts echoing Max Weber,[6] states :

> There is no point at which any of the doctrines of nibbanic Buddhism articulates with the secular social order, either to give it value, on the one hand, or to provide a fulcrum by which it can be changed on the other.[7]
>
> ...the only emotional state ultimately valued by nibbanic Buddhism — [is] that of detachment (*upekkhā*). Ultimately,

> the behavior of the true Buddhist (unlike, say, the true Christian) is governed not by love but by detachment.[8]

Spiro, in speaking of detachment (*upekkhā*), refers to the sublime attitude equanimity to which he ascribes the meaning of (a) emotional detachment with respect to both one's own fate and the fate of others and (b) the destruction of all emotion.[9] Thus, according to King and Spiro, serious practitioners of Buddhism — monks and lay meditators — practice nibbanic Buddhism in contrast to kammatic Buddhism. To paraphrase King and Spiro, they have withdrawn from society seeking the realization of nirvāṇa which will leave them with the sublime attitude equanimity, the destruction of emotion. Such individuals will have no effect on society.

The division of Theravāda Buddhism into nibbanic and kammatic Buddhism is doctrinally unfounded. While it is true that the teachings on liberation from rebirth are considered more profound than those on achieving high rebirth, the former are not totally distinct from the latter. Practitioners of insight, the so-called nibbanic Buddhists, are still very much working within the laws of cause (*kamma*) and effect. The cultivation of virtuous activities (*kamma*) insures good rebirth, but more importantly creates the nexus within which a practitioner can cultivate concentration and insight in the present.

The profound path of insight is the eightfold noble path — right speech, action, livelihood, effort, mindfulness, concentration, direction, view. The first three aspects of this path pertain to correct conduct, the next three to concentration and the last two to wisdom — correct conduct, concentration, and wisdom being called the Buddhist threefold training. If one, undertaking the first training, neither harms nor deceives others, then one's activities (*kamma*) are conducive to an absence of remorse for misdeeds and to consequent happiness. If one makes effort in the cultivation of wholesome physical, verbal, and mental activities (*kamma*), is mindful of one's actions and thoughts, and sharpens the mind with the second training of concentration, one attains mental control and satisfaction. If one is free from hate as well as harmfulness and cultivates the third training leading to correct understanding of reality, one can uproot the causes of future rebirth and its attendant suffering.

The three trainings, though sequential, mutually reinforce each other.[10] For, the concentrated controlled individual quite naturally inclines to correct conduct and is quick to achieve insight while one with wisdom sees the benefits of correct activities and the quickest ways to attain concentration. Similarly, sympathy motivates correct conduct to others, concentration on the sublime attitudes, and the cultivation of insight, while such concentration and insight serve to deepen and purify sympathy which in turn motivates activity (*kamma*) for others. There is no unbridgeable breach between the "nibbanic" and "kammic," rather a mutually supportive mesh of the two. Such a relationship of love, compassion, sympathetic joy, and equanimity to each other in meditation, to the cultivation of insight, and to activity subsequent to insight has been misunderstood by Spiro and King, resulting in their bifurcated vision of Theravāda Buddhism.

According to Theravāda tradition, the Bodhisattva (the being who in an earlier life vowed to become Gotama Buddha) had to cultivate virtue for a vast period of time, during the course of many lives, to give his mind the ability to realize the four truths without the guidance of a teacher. He cultivated virtuous activities (*kamma*) such as gift giving to the needy (of obvious social impact) in order ultimately to realize nirvāṇa. He was motivated by the wish to help others. On a smaller scale, the same is true for every disciple who follows Gotama. An individual needs to have accumulated virtuous activities to come into contact with the Buddhist religion; then, he must continue to cultivate and sustain virtue throughout his practice in order to create the proper setting for the development of concentration and insight; and he should be motivated in his practice by a wish for others' welfare (see pp. 17-18). In their statements King and Spiro abstract the practice of insight from its actual behavioral and attitudinal context — a broad spectrum of virtuous activities, as well as a concern for self and others.

A fully liberated individual has destroyed the seeds of future rebirth; furthermore, his intentions no longer have the ability to entail rebirth, technically speaking, his intentions are no longer karmic.[11] This liberated condition, however, is obtained by working within the context of wholesome intentions and deeds (*kamma*) and it is thus misleading to contrast "kammatic

Buddhism" with "nibbanic Buddhism." Meditators seeking nirvāṇa engage in activities similar to those undertaken by those seeking high rebirth — correct conduct, generosity, and concentration — and in addition cultivate insight. They do not constitute a different kind of Buddhism, rather a more complete level of practice.

In examining equanimity as an ethical ideal, one finds the term occurring in a variety of contexts in the discourses with clearly different but unarticulated shades of meaning. Buddhaghoṣa's *Path of Purification* isolates ten distinct meanings of "equanimity" in the discourses and commentaries, giving analytical definitions for each. Six types of equanimity relevant to this discussion shed light on King and Spiro's assertions.

The feeling of equanimity. The "feeling equanimity" (*vedanā-upekkhā*) is the experience of neither pain nor pleasure (Vism.iv. 162) and can arise in wholesome, unwholesome, and neutral states of mind. Wholesome states of mind are associated with either the feeling of mental pleasure or equanimity (Vism.xiv.83). For example, if out of generosity one gives a gift to an inspiring religious teacher, one is likely to have a wholesome generous even mind associated with the feeling of mental pleasure (Vism.xiv.84). On the other hand, if one gives the same gift to a lackluster monk, one is likely to have a similar mind but associated with the feeling of equanimity (Vism.xiv.85).

Unwholesome states of mind are divided into three categories — states of attachment, aversion, or delusion (Vism.xiv.89). Attached states of mind are associated with either the feeling of mental pleasure or equanimity (Vism.xiv.90). For example, the attachment connected with finding a jewel on the street is likely to be associated with a feeling of mental pleasure, whereas that connected with finding a small coin on the street is likely to be associated with no more than a feeling of equanimity (Vism. xiv.91).

Aversive states are always conjoined with the feeling of mental suffering/grief (Vism.xiv.92), and deluded states are always associated with the feeling equanimity (Vism.xiv.93). In chart form this is :

State of Mind	Associated Feeling		
	Mental Pleasure	Mental Suffering	Equanimity
I. Wholesome	Possible	Impossible	Possible
II. Unwholesome			
a. Attachment	Possible	Impossible	Possible
b. Aversion	Impossible	Necessarily	Impossible
c. Delusion	Impossible	Impossible	Necessarily

These represent the feelings associated with our common reactions, whereas practitioners cultivating concentration successively achieve the uncommon states of mind called "the absorptions" (*jhāna*). The first three of these are associated with bliss; the fourth, with the feeling equanimity (Vism.xiv.86). Since when a practitioner realizes nirvāṇa, his mind is at the level of one of the four absorptions, the realization of it is associated with either the feeling of bliss or equanimity (Vism.xiv.158).

Even-minded equanimity. "Even-minded equanimity" (*tatra-majjhatta-upekkhā*) is the mental factor/attitude which "conducts the mind and [its co-arisen] mental factors evenly" (Vism.iv.164; xiv.153). This attitude "hinders deficiency and excess" (Vism. xiv.153), and "looks on the mind and [its co-arisen] mental factors as a charioteer looks on [his] evenly progressing thoroughbreds" (Vism.xiv.153). This is the attitude in a wholesome mind which maintains and observes the balance of the other attitudes present. By one name or another it is present in every wholesome state of mind (Vism.xiv.156-158). A corollary of this is that nonvirtuous states of mind are characterized by an absence of balance and the presence of agitation to one degree or another (Vism.xiv.160-78).

Equanimity in the sense of balance is a wholesome conditioning mental-factor/attitude (*saṅkhāra*). Thus, it can be understood that an individual creates this attitude in dependence on previous familiarity with it and that present familiarization with it will serve as a condition for its generation in the future. This conditioning mental factor is functionally distinct from the feeling equanimity since it maintains an evenness of attitude whereas the latter is the experience of neither pain nor pleasure. This distinction is illustrated in the case of a generous act. An individual who gives a gift to another has a wholesome generous even mind (Vism.xiv.84-85, 156). He possesses even-minded equanimity whether he gives the gift to an ordinary monk and has the *feeling* equanimity or he gives the gift to a more inspiring monk and has the feeling of pleasure. Having a wholesome mind, his responses are balanced, whether his feeling is equanimous or pleasurable.

The next four types of equanimity are various forms of even-mindedness (Vism.iv.167), given individual names because they occur on different occasions. It is like one individual who at various times in his life is called "young man," "general," "king," and so forth. Since the five kinds of even-mindedness are contextually distinct, they are mutually exclusive (Vism.iv.167).

Equanimity of purity. "Equanimity of purity" (*parisuddhi-upekkhā*) is the equanimity associated with the fourth absorption (Vism.iv.166). In the first three absorptions even-mindedness is needed to balance four predominant mental factors : initial application of mind (*vitakka*), sustained application of mind (*vicāra*), pleasurable interest (*pīti*), and bliss (*sukha*). Buddhaghoṣa explains that in the first three absorptions even-minded equanimity resembles the crescent moon which occurs during the day and is neither pure nor clear because it is overpowered by the radiance of the sun and is lacking the assistance of its ally the night (Vism. iv.195). In the first three absorptions, the crescent moon of even-mindedness is not pure because it is overpowered by the limbs of absorption — initial application of mind, and so forth— and because it is without the assistance of its ally, the feeling equanimity.

The fourth absorption is unique because even-minded equanimity is accompanied by the feeling equanimity which clarifies the former. (The first three absorptions are associated with the feeling of bliss thereby precluding the feeling equanimity). In the fourth absorption, the crescent moon of even-minded equanimity is pure because it is not outshone by the mental factors of initial application of mind, and so forth, and because it is accompanied by its ally the feeling equanimity.

The sublime attitude equanimity. The "sublime attitude equanimity" (*brahmavihāra-upekkhā*) is a combination of both an even functioning of the mind and its associated mental factors, as well as an even or neutral attitude towards others — friend, foe and neutral. The sublime attitude equanimity is free from the dangers associated with the first three sublime attitudes (see above pp. 64-66), it is peaceful (*śāntabhāva*, Vism.ix.88), and it is endowed with all the virtues of equanimity of purity differing from the latter only in relation to the type of object they each have. The sublime attitude occurs in relation to sentient beings (Vism.iv.102); the equanimity of purity, to a bright internal image called the counterpart sign (Vism.iv.31, 181).

The limb of enlightenment equanimity. The "limb of enlightenment equanimity" (*bojjhaṅga-uppekkhā*) is the balance among the constituents of the mind which realizes nirvāṇa (Vism.iv.159). Seven mental factors are singled out in discussions of the realization of nirvāṇa — mindfulness (*sati*), investigation of phenomena (*dhammavicaya*), energy (*viriya*), pleasurable interest (*pīti*), tranquillity (*passaddhi*), concentration (*samādhi*), and equanimity (*upekkhā*). Because the simultaneous occurrence of these seven factors with nirvāṇa as their object constitutes enlightenment (MA.i.289), they are called the limbs of enlightenment.

Depending on the strength of a meditator's concentration, he will realize nirvāṇa with a mind at the level of any one of the four absorptions (Vism.xiv.158).[12] The realization of nirvāṇa with a mind at the level of one of the first *three* absorptions would be blissful; thus, pleasurable interest and bliss can occur during the realization of nirvāṇa but these are protected from attachment by the limb of enlightenment equanimity. Part of the meditator's training is to learn how to maintain an even attitude in the face of the pleasurable interest and bliss which occur in the cultivation of insight and can easily lead to attachment (Vism.xx.105-130).

Six-limbed equanimity. "Six limbed equanimity" (*chaḷaṅga-upekkhā*) consists of not abandoning mental purity with regard to desired or undesired objects which might appear to any of the six senses (Vism.iv.157). Only fully liberated individuals, Buddhas and Worthy Ones, maintain such an unbroken continuum of even-mindedness. It is important to note here that such persons do not abandon pleasurable emotion; they do, however, maintain even-mindedness or mental balance while experiencing such feelings as pleasure or bliss (Vism.xiv.109).

Scriptural Description of a Fully Liberated Being

Buddha presents the virtues which make a fully liberated individual worthy of respect, stating, "[When] he sees form with his eye, he becomes neither mentally pleased, nor mentally displeased, but remains equanimous, mindful, and discriminating [and so on for all six senses]" (A.iii.279).[13] On the surface this description seems to support Spiro's characterization of the Buddhist ideal as the destruction of emotion. It may even be that this passage helped generate Spiro's theory since it seems to indicate that fully liberated individuals are without the affects of pleasure or displeasure and that they maintain equanimity. However, it is important to identify which type of equanimity is intended here. The commentary does just this, thereby shedding light on the overall meaning of the passage :

> *Neither mentally pleased nor mentally displeased*, he does not become mentally pleased with regard to a desired object due to the mental pleasure which arises with attachment, nor does he become mentally displeased with regard to an undesired object due to the mental displeasure which arises with hatred.
>
> *He remains equanimous, mindful and discriminating*, he does not attain equanimity with regard to a neutral object due to unknowing equanimity which is an absence of consideration. [Rather] having become mindful and discriminating, he remains even-minded with regard to the object.
>
> In this discourse, the continuous state of one who has destroyed all the harmful influences [one fully liberated] is explained. (AA.iii.335)

The commentary first delineates the types of experiences a fully liberated person cannot have — the pleasure which arises with attachment, the displeasure which arises with aversion, and the equanimity (indifference) which arises due to unknowing equanimity (*aññāṇaupekkhā*). The disparaging usage of "equanimity" as indifference and the phrase "unknowing equanimity" are both unaccounted for in the seemingly exhaustive analysis of equanimity in *The Path of Purification* (Vism.iv.156-170). However, Dhammapāla, the sixth century commentator to *The Path of Purification*, explains that unknowing equanimity is *ignorance* dissociated from feelings of mental pleasure and displeasure,[14] in other words possessed of the feeling equanimity. Since the above quoted commentary explains that fully liberated individuals are free from attachment, aversion, and *ignorance* as well as the pleasure, displeasure, and equanimity respectively associated with them, the enduring equanimity mentioned in the discourse cannot possibly refer to the dull absence of emotion suggested by Spiro.

Buddhas and Worthy Ones have abandoned all defiled attitudes and their associated feelings; their responses are characterized by balance or evenness. Buddhaghoṣa's commentary clearly refers to six-limbed equanimity as the referent for the discourse passage. This is distinct in meaning from the feeling equanimity and the sublime attitude and is not necessarily accompanied by a neutral feeling. Possessed of this even-mindedness, fully liberated beings have a whole spectrum of attitudinal responses open to them, such as cultivating concentrated love with its associated feeling of bliss. Such persons are not unemotional. Their emotions can be outgoing and joyous, yet always even and pure.

Separate Meanings

It seems that Winston King has also made an incorrect identification assuming that the sublime attitude equanimity is the limb of enlightenment equanimity. Therefore let us look into these in more detail.

The Sublime Attitude Equanimity

The cultivation of the sublime attitude equanimity is one of many forms of concentration taught by the Buddha. A practitioner might be moved to cultivate it from the advice of his teacher or his own estimation of the rewards it offers. This attitude is said to be especially effective for the suppression of aversion and lust (M.i.424, D.iii.248). Successful cultivation brings such worldly benefits as peaceful sleep, pleasurable dreams, and rebirth in the satisfying world of Brahma (Vism.ix.83). (These worldly benefits are also obtainable through the successful cultivation of the first three sublime attitudes). In addition, the sublime attitude equanimity is conducive to the development of the factors of mind necessary for the realization of nirvāṇa (above, p. 84).

Of the four sublime attitudes, equanimity is the most potent in terms of helping a practitioner develop the limb of enlightenment equanimity which is necessary for the realization of nirvāṇa.[15] The sublime attitude equanimity, coming as it does at the level of the fourth absorption, would familiarize the practitioner with pure even-mindedness and thus be most conducive to producing the balance necessary for realizing nirvāṇa. Since the other sublime attitudes are developed in the first three absorptions, they are less conducive to the development of such balance.[16]

It is clear that the sublime attitude equanimity has virtues and characteristics that set it apart and distinguish it from the first three sublime attitudes. Nevertheless, it is not the case that these distinguishing characteristics make this attitude qualitatively of a different order from the first three sublime attitudes as King suggests when he says, "With upekkhā, or [the sublime attitude] equanimity, considered to be the crown and fruition of the other aspects [namely, the other sublime attitudes], one moves definitely into the realm of nibbanic ethic."[17]

We can grant that in so far as both the sublime attitude equanimity and nirvāṇa are called peaceful there is an homology between the former state of mind and the latter supramundane condition (Vism.ix.88; S.iv.368). We can also accept that in so far as the sublime attitude equanimity is more potent for the development of the limb of enlightenment variety it would be more conducive for the realization of nirvāṇa. However, this does not lead to the conclusion that the sublime attitude equanimity is in a relationship to nirvāṇa, or its realization, which makes it qualitatively distinct from the first three sublime attitudes. The first three sublime attitudes, being virtuous states of mind, are associated with tranquillity (*passadhi*, Vism.xiv.157); thus, they too would be homologous with nirvāṇa to some extent. Furthermore, as was pointed out above, the superiority of the sublime attitude equanimity in generating the limb of enlightenment equanimity is a matter of degree, not of kind.

In part, King presents what a close analysis of the texts and commentaries indicate, namely, that the sublime attitude equanimity is similar in character to nirvāṇa and causally significant for its realization. Unfortunately, he does not mention the similar virtues of the first three sublime attitudes. Exaggerating the uniqueness and hence the value of the sublime attitude equanimity, he compounds the error by mistakenly identifying the sublime attitude equanimity with the limb of enlightenment equanimity, adding the normative value of the latter to the former.[18]

The assertion that the sublime attitude equanimity is qualitatively distinct from the other sublime attitudes also obscures the fact that these four attitudes are to be developed together in a complementary relationship to one another.[19] Just as parents have love, compassion, and sympathetic joy for their children in their youth and equanimity toward them when they become independent and involved in their own affairs, so too a meditator first develops the concerned attitudes of love, compassion, and sympathetic joy and then complements these with the neutrality of equanimity (see above, p. 70).[20]

This analogy between parents and a meditator is useful for clarifying the complementary nature of the four sublime attitudes, but it creates the wrong impression that just as parents who have completed rearing their children continuously adopt a more or less equanimous attitude to them, so too a practiced meditator would maintain an equanimous attitude to beings in (or out of) meditation. This is not the case. Achieving skill in the cultivation of equanimity means that one has culminated one's *training* in the four sublime attitudes, but not that equanimity is to supplant the first three sublime attitudes in one's future practice. Rather, one is to develop skill in all four sublime attitudes and continue to reiterate the practice of all four of them. Gotama, who was skilled in the sublime attitude equanimity, continued to cultivate all four sublime attitudes after his enlightenment (A.i.181). He never indicates that the fourth one should supercede the first three. If we were to speculate on why Buddha still engaged in these meditations after his enlightenment, we would have to give the answer he often gave regarding the motives behind his behavior—

personal satisfaction in the present and sympathy for the people of the future (see above p. 7).

Equanimity can be understood to be the peaceful but temporary complement to the first three more concerned dispositions. Before one has forever abandoned mental defilements, the four attitudes are useful as antidotes to four different unwholesome factors (see above p. 63). Though after enlightenment one's mind is no longer in danger of becoming unwholesome (see above p. 73), each attitude would be capable of offering the rewards unique to themselves and their level of absorption.

King is aware of the complementary nature of the sublime attitudes,[21] but neglects this important facet when he gives the misleading impression that the attainment of equanimity leaves one free from any interest in the first three and devoid of concern for others. He states :

> Whatever [English] term we adopt [for *upekkhā*], something of its quality is evident : controlled balance of mind, emotional non-attachment or neutrality, and 'beyondness' with regard to ordinary ethical uncertainties and struggles. It is seemingly a calm detachment of eternity mindedness that has little interest longer in the ordinary affairs of men; ......the possessor of equanimity goes on, completely unshaken emotionally or mentally by the world's mental, moral, or social disturbances.[22]

Here, it is fitting to consider Gotama as he was skilled in this attitude (A.i.183). He did not turn his back on the concerns of the common man. He spent the last forty-five years of his life wandering to different parts of India teaching individuals from all walks of life assorted topics including those relating to the "ordinary affairs of men" such as gambling, investment, and conjugal relations.[23] King's generalization with regard to the consequences of the sublime attitude equanimity does not stand up to the evidence.

His interpretation brings into focus the need for understanding the relationship of the four sublime attitudes to each other both in terms of meditation and daily life. Both King and Spiro have mis-characterized Theravāda Buddhism because they have assumed that the traditional praise of the *psychological* virtues of the sublime attitude equanimity in meditation prescribe an ethic of neutrality outside of meditation. However, once we have understood that practitioners maintain the practice of all four sublime attitudes even after their enlightenment, it is important to explore just how these attitudes carry over to daily life. We might expect all four sublime attitudes to exert an equal effect on meditators outside of meditation, but if each was of a similar force, how could a practitioner be equally impelled to love and neutrality? What would be the resultant attitude ?

In fact, such an equal blend of all four attitudes is unthinkable. Because sympathy for others is supposed to motivate the whole religious life including the cultivation of sublime attitudes, it is implicit that the effects arising from the cultivation of the sublime attitudes are to be weighted in such a way as to sustain sympathy.[24] Thus, the first three sublime attitudes exert a controlling influence on a practitioner's behavior outside of meditation; the last attitude, a qualifying effect. Love, compassion, and sympathetic joy enrich the practitioner's sympathy for others; equanimity, the practitioner's evenness of mind. In conclusion, the sublime attitude equanimity is not meant to leave the practitioner with an attitude of neutrality outside of meditation. It is clear from the example of Gotama that unbiased concern is to be the ethical norm in Theravāda (S.i.206, 111) and that such an attitude is achievable through emphasizing the components of the sublime attitudes in the above way. Because the four sublime attitudes each contribute something to sustaining, enriching, and equalizing sympathy, all four recommend themselves to practitioners.

The Limb of Enlightenment Equanimity

There is much prescriptive material in the Theravāda canon urging practitioners to realize nirvāṇa. Its full realization entails permanent liberation from all attachment, hatred, and delusion; and, at death, freedom from rebirth and its attendant sufferings. When one realizes nirvāṇa, the seven limbs of enlightenment are predominant. Thus, it could be said that the goal in cultivating insight is the simultaneous achievement of all *seven* limbs of enlightenment with nirvāṇa as their object.

It is something of a distortion to single out the limb of enlighten ment equanimity, as King has done, as the ethical ideal of

Buddhism. There is, however, an even broader problem. Is a practitioner's personal liberation from mental defilement and the freedom from rebirth it entails the ethical ideal of Buddhism, or is this goal embedded in a broader ethical context ?

If we look first at the life of Buddha, we see that he became enlightened (*buddha*, realized nirvāṇa) in order to help others (see above, p. 3). Four innumerable and a hundred thousand aeons before the birth of Gotama, an ascetic named Sumedha conceived the aspiration to achieve Buddhahood — an aspiration which was realized in his much later rebirth as Gotama.[25] Sumedha is said to have had the capacity to achieve liberation as a Worthy One in his lifetime.[26] However, having become impressed with Buddha Dīpaṃkara, he abandoned all concern for immediate liberation and instead vowed to become a Buddha[27] — a being who would reintroduce the helpful teaching of the four noble truths when they were no longer known in the world.[28] When Gotama finally became enlightened, he benefited himself, but his primary motivation was an altruistic concern to benefit others by exemplifying and teaching the religious way of life that had disappeared from the world.

For practitioners Buddha stated three types of acceptable motivations. He said it was fitting to make effort if they see some benefit to (a) themselves, (b) others, or (c) both (A.iv.134-35). Context demands that we understand "benefit" (*attha*) to mean religious benefit in this instance. At first glance, it would seem that Buddha was willing for practitioners to have either egocentric, altruistic, or hybrid (egocentric/altruistic) motivations. However, Buddha's later exhortation to the monks in his final days at Vesāli to undertake their own realization of nirvāṇa out of concern for others' well being (see above p. 17) indicates that Gotama wanted practitioners ultimately to have altruistic or at least hybrid motivations. Practitioners should undertake training in morality, concentration, and insight with an eye to the benefits that this undertaking will bring to others. Meditators can helpfully affect others through the inspiring model of their conduct and transmission of the doctrine.

On the basis of Gotama's description of his own motivation and on the basis of his exhortation to the monks at Vesāli it seems fitting to characterize the ethical structure of Theravāda Buddhism as either altruistic or hybrid (egocentric/altruistic). We can interpret the isolated instances of egocentric exhortations as being intended for flagging practitioners who were not even capable of seeking their own welfare, let alone that of others. Once such practitioners achieved some personal progress, they would be expected to broaden their sphere of concern and practice with either an altruistic or hybrid motivation. This assessment is supported by the Theravāda precept against suicide (Vin.iii.82); Buddha, mindful of the benefits his disciples could bring others, proscribed suicide (Miln.195-196). Thus, no matter what their initial motives were, practitioners should ultimately live within a recognition of the benefits they convey to others. The realization of nirvāṇa (which involves the limb of enlightenment equanimity) as well as practitioners' subsequent conduct are inextricably linked with concern for others. This belies King's characterization of the limb of enlightenment as entailing "little interest longer in the ordinary affairs of men."[29]

It is worthwhile to investigate briefly material that may have caused King to come to his conclusion. One of the techniques for generating the limb of enlightenment equanimity is the cultivation of neutrality with regard to sentient beings (Vism.iv.62), though not necessarily in meditative absorption.[30] This neutrality in turn is engendered by reflecting that (a) beings are heirs to their own deeds and (b) in the ultimate sense there are no sentient beings. When these reflections are well cultivated, they lead to the evenness of mind necessary for realization of nirvāṇa, at which time the object of one's mind is nirvāṇa, not sentient beings (P.P.xiv.nt.67). By limiting consideration to the second of the above reflections and to the absence of beings in the realization of nirvāṇa, one might assume, as King does, that there is not much room for concern towards others in Theravāda. Moreover, it could be argued that if the conceptual understanding of selflessness is conducive to neutrality towards others, then the profound realization of selflessness associated with the direct cognition of nirvāṇa should definitively establish neutrality as the ethical attitude subsequent to enlightenment.[31]

These arguments raise two distinct but related questions. Does the realization of selflessness allow a subsequent relation with others ? What ethical attitudes would be consonant with this realization ? Buddhaghoṣa's instructions on cultivating the sublime attitude love present material relevant to both questions

(Vism.ix.38). When a person tries to develop love with regard to a hostile individual, anger may arise. In order to abandon this anger and cultivate love, the practitioner is counseled to consider that in the ultimate sense beings do not exist. This is aimed at weeding out mental imbalance. Unwholesome reactions toward others cannot survive the wholesome analytical realization that in the ultimate sense there are no sentient beings. The first step in this procedure involves investigating the momentary mental and physical constituents of the object in search of the locus for one's anger. The locus, being the person with whom one is angry, cannot be found in any of the mental or physical phenomena such as hair, skin, eye consciousness, ear consciousness, and so forth (Vism.ix.38). One comes to realize that in the ultimate sense there is no person (Vism.xviii.28). This realization, occurring in a wholesome state of mind, is associated with evenness of mind; hence, at this point one would have succeeded in abandoning anger.

In the next step the meditator, sustaining evenmindedness, reestablishes the hostile individual as the object of his mind and adopts a neutral attitude. The meditation does not stop with selflessness. Though the Theravādins did not articulate the philosophical justification behind the provisional acceptance of conventional realities, such as sentient beings, which are ultimately nonexistent, it is clear that such is practically possible as is evidenced by the example of Buddha. He realized that in the ultimate sense there is no self, but subsequently, possessing this understanding, he went on to act on behalf of provisionally accepted other selves. Similarly the cultivator of love, having established a wholesome neutral attitude toward the provisionally accepted hostile individual, proceeds to develop love. Maintaining his evenness of mind and dropping his neutrality, he wishes for the other's welfare.

It can thus be seen that the understanding of selflessness, though conducive to neutrality, does not preclude positive concern for others' happiness. This is further confirmed by the contemporary Burmese meditation master U Satyanarayan Goenka who has stated that the realization of nirvāṇa facilitates an attitude of love towards others.[32] The discourses and commentaries do not explicitly discuss the relationships between the realization of nirvāṇa and subsequent attitudes towards others, but it appears that any neutrality prompted through insight is naturally, as a matter of course, replaced by a wholesome interest in others (see above, p. 16). Though there is an apparent tension between the inclination to neutrality due to the realization of selflessness and the natural sentiment of concern for others, this tension seems to dissolve experientially. This view is supported by the extensive textual material concerning Gotama's active involvement with others and U Goenka's testimony.

In concluding this analysis of King's characterization of Theravāda let us briefly look at the nature of meditative retreats in Theravāda Buddhism. We have already established that both meditation and teaching are to be undertaken with an eye to others' benefit. There are no strict timetables set on how practitioners are to arrange their commitments to these two activities, but if we look at the accounts of Gotama's life, we see that he spent six years in semi-isolation before his enlightenment. Afterwards, he alternated teaching and meditation with meditative retreats that lasted from a portion of a day up to two weeks.[33] All accounts indicate that there has always been a rich variety in the religious life in terms of the amount of time individuals would allot to silent contemplation and teaching.[34] The image of a play between activity and retreat that emerges is quite different from the unidirectional once and for all "withdrawal from the active life of historical involvement" which according to King typifies monastic Buddhism.[35] Even a cursory investigation of the discourses reveals many lengthy contacts between Buddha and the leaders of his day.[36] Similarly, a perusal of the historical records reveals extensive and active involvement by monks in the societies where Buddhism has established itself, primarily in education.[37]

King in his characterization of Theravāda Buddhism has taken certain aspects of equanimity and generalized them beyond their range of applicability. The error has been magnified by his failure to take account of the large amount of descriptive and prescriptive material in the canon on the altruistic contextualization of practice and the varied nature of the religious life.

Detachment or Concern

Spiro's choice of "detachment" (*upekkhā*) as the ultimate value of Theravāda Buddhism is inaccurate and confusing. First of all, if "detachment" means the sublime attitude equanimity, as he indicates,[38] then it has already been shown that this is not the most highly valued attitude in Theravāda Buddhism (see pp. 89-90). Buddha and his followers did not limit themselves to an attitude of neutrality with regard to beings, nor did they ever assert that this is the only or even the best attitude to have.

In identifying "detachment" as the destruction of all emotion Spiro is apparently merging several distinct Buddhist concepts into one unfounded unit. It seems that he has taken the limb of enlightenment equanimity which is efficacious for abandoning negative attitudes or emotions such as hatred,[39] combined it with six-limbed equanimity which is the continuous pure balance of the fully enlightened, added in the experiential neutrality of the feeling equanimity as well as the attitudinal neutrality of the sublime attitude equanimity, and come up with a supposedly highly valued super-equanimity which has neither doctrinal equivalent nor theoretical validity.[40] For, although fully liberated beings have abandoned all the negative emotions of attachment, hatred, and delusion, they have not destroyed *all* emotion and feeling. They have the ability to develop a whole range of rich and satisfying emotions and are encouraged in scripture to do so.[41]

Spiro goes on to say that the ideal act in Buddhism is governed by this detachment. Insofar as he identifies "detachment" as the sublime attitude equanimity, he is wrong since nowhere is this extolled as the guiding light of Buddhist activity. Rather, the ideal act, embodied in the personage of the fully liberated one, is *accompanied* by six-limbed equanimity. This is the pure balance that accompanies such a person's responses to situations and sentient beings, whether he be responding with insight, joy, or kindness. In the light of what has been said above about Buddha's own benevolence and his exhortations to the monks, it would be far more fitting to assert that the ideal act in Buddhism is governed by concern for others' happiness and welfare.

In sum, although there are scriptural sources indicating that fully liberated individuals continuously maintain equanimity, the commentaries explained that the equanimity intended here is the six-limbed variety, namely, a pure balance of mind in the face of desired or undesired objects. This balance can accompany the whole gamut of attitudinal responses that are normally associated with a wholesome mind.

It is thus important here to avoid establishing an amorphous and impossible combination of the limb of enlightenment equanimity, the sublime attitude equanimity, the feeling equanimity and six-limbed equanimity and making this the ultimate attitude of Theravāda Buddhism. To claim that this attitude is the goal of those seeking full liberation and the cause for monks' purported withdrawal from contact with society further compounds the error. According to this view Buddhists would ideally sustain neutrality towards one another and experience only the feeling of neither-pleasure-nor-pain.

The discourses, commentaries, and historical records, however, indicate a different picture of the ethical ideal of Theravāda Buddhism as well as the results of its practice. Gotama, the paradigm of practice, followed an altruistic ethical ideal and exhorted his disciples to do the same. Motivated by an interest in others' well-being, he achieved enlightenment and went on to be involved with society through his teaching. He was capable of a wide range of attitudes and feelings : a man with kindness, concern, and joy. Gotama actively shared his insights, touched others' hearts, and moved them to follow him. To the present this model has animated and inspired Theravāda Buddhism.

NOTE ON REFERENCES

In general when I have referred to canonical texts by title, I have used the titles of the English translations in the Pali Text Society translation series. When giving references, I have given page numbers for the Pali text of the Pali Text Society editions of the canon. Almost all the canonical works are available in Pali Text Society translations. These translations are cross-referenced with the original Pali, so that a reference to the page number of a Pali text is easily found in its translation.

References to the *Upaniṣads* are to chapter, section, and sub-section.

References to the *Visuddhimagga* are to chapter, and section. These references are easily found in its translation *The Path of Purification.*

NOTES

Introduction

1. There is a standard set of instructions for cultivating these four attitudes collectively (D.i.250, discussed below in Chapter Five passim). Outside the context of these instructions, only love receives significant independent attention. In such independent instances, if love is universal and at the level of absorption it can be considered a sublime attitude.

2. I have also referred to material from the fifth collection of discourses when such reference was appropriate. In addition to the discourse basket (*piṭaka*), the Buddhist canon is made up of the discipline (*vinaya*) basket and the higher doctrine (*abhidhamma*) basket. I have alluded to material from these parts of the canon when necessary.

3. A. D. Pusalker, "Religion and Philosophy : The Pali Canon," *History and Culture of the Indian People*, 2nd ed., general ed. R. C. Majumdar (Bombay : Bharatiya Vidya Bhavan, 1953), II : 408.

4. L. R. Goonasekere, *Buddhist Commentarial Literature*, The Wheel Publication, 113 (Kandy : Buddhist Publication Society, 1967), p. 15.

5. *Ibid.*, pp. 3, 11-12.

6. *Ibid.*, p. 12.

7. Buddhaghoṣa, *Visuddhimagga*, ed. Henry Clark Warren. Harvard Oriental Series, 41 (Cambridge : Harvard University Press, 1950). This is available in an excellent translation as *The Path of Purification*, trans. Bhikkhu Ñāṇamoli, 2nd ed. (Colombo : A. Semage, 1964). After being out of print for several years, it is now available from Shambhala Publications, Berkeley, California.

8. Winston King, *In the Hope of Nibbana : Theravada Buddhist Ethics* (La Salle : Open Court, 1964), p. 168; and Melford Spiro, *Buddhism and Society : A Great Tradition and Its Burmese Vicissitudes* (New York : Harper Paperbacks, 1972), p. 427.

9. One work that gives testimony to the contribution of the monastic community to its host society is Walpola Rahula's *The Heritage of the Bhikkhu : A Short History of the Bhikkhu in Educational Cultural, Social, and Political Life*, trans. K. P. G. Wijayasurendra (New York : Grove Press, 1974).

Chapter One

1. C. A. F. Rhys Davids offers "to vibrate towards, or after" as an etymological definition of *anukampā*. *See* C. A. F. Rhys Davids, "Love (Buddhist), "in *Encyclopedia of Religion and Ethics*, ed. James Hasting (New York : Charles Scribner's Sons, 1916), 8:159-62.

2. *anukampā ti mettāya pubba-bhāga* (DA.ii.456). *See* W. G. Weeraratne, "Anukampā," in *Encyclopedia of Buddhism*, ed. G. P. Malalasekera (Government of Ceylon, 1967), fascicle 4:742.

3. "Sympathy for the world" means sympathy for the world of beings. *Lokānukampakāya* (sic) *sattalokassa anukampaṃ* (AA.i.100).

4. *See also*, the "Discourse on the Marks" (D.iii.148-49, 154, 164).

5. The paths (*magga*) and fruitions (*phala*), which occur just for one brief period at each level of realization, are mentioned in the discourses and receive extensive discussion in the commentaries (Vism.chap.xxii). The "Fruition-attainment" (*phala-samāpatti*) is the re-experience of the fruition state outside the sequence of realizing the paths. For example, once a practitioner has experienced the path and fruition of Stream-Entering, he can, in a subsequent period of meditation, re-experience the fruition-consciousness of a Stream-Enterer, without, however, re-experiencing the path consciousness of a Stream-Enterer. This state is not mentioned in the discourses, but is discussed at length in the commentaries (Vism.xxiii.1-15).

6. For Buddha's identification of his motives *see* M.i.46; M.i.188; iii.302; S.iv.359, 361, 373; v. 157; A.iii.87, 89; iv. 139.

7. G. P. Malalasekera, *Dictionary of Pali Proper Names*, 2 vols. (London : Pali Text Society, 1969), 2:613.

8. Any act of knowing (*viññaṇa*) involves mind (*citta*) and mental factors (*cetasika*). Whereas the mind is the basic knower, the mental factors are the discrete functions which give the mind its different characterization at different times. Each mental factor is a discrete entity. There are some mental factors that are common to every state of mind (*sabbacittasādhāraṇā*). There are others that occur miscellaneously (*pakiṇṇakā*) in wholesome or unwholesome states of mind. There are unwholesome mental factors, some of which occur in every unwholesome state, and others which occur only occasionally. The same is the case with wholesome mental factors. The mental factors alluded to in the text are a sample of mental factors that could co-arise and motivate an individual to action without attachment. Intention (*cetanā*) and concentration (*samādhi* or *ekaggatā*) are two of the mental factors that occur in every state of mind. (The concentration in unwholesome states is very weak, Vism.xiv.177). Initial application of the mind to an object (*vitakka*), sustained application of the mind to an object (*vicāra*), energy (*viriya*), inclination to act (*chanda*), and decision (*adhimokkha*) are five of the miscellaneous factors that can occur in association with various states of mind. Flexibility (*mudutā*), adaptability (*kammaññutā*) and proficiency (*paguññatā*) are three of the wholesome mental factors which occur in association with every wholesome state of mind. Abstention from wrong activity (*kāyaduccaritavirati*), abstention from wrong speech (*vacīduccaritavirati*), abstention from wrong livelihood (*micchājīvavirati*) are three of the wholesome mental factors that sometimes accompany a wholesome state of mind. *See* Vism.xiv.133-184; Nārada Mahā Thera, *A Manual of Abhidhamma : being Abhidhammattha Sangaha* (Kandy : Buddhist Publication Society, 1968), pp. 78-141; Lama Anagarika Govinda, *The Psychological Attitude of Early Buddhist Philosophy* (London : Rider and Company, 1969), pp. 115-24, 149.

9. On the distinctions between wholesome and unwholesome mental factors see Vism.xiv.133-78. On ways of experiencing the differences between mental factors see D.ii.300-304; Nyanaponika-Thera, *The Heart of Buddhist Meditation* (London : Rider and Company, 1969), pp. 125-28;

Nyanaponika-Thera, *The Power of Mindfulness* (San Francisco : Unity Press, 1972); Mahasi Sayadaw, *Practical Insight Meditation* (San Francisco : Unity Press, 1972); Soma-Thera, *The Way of Mindfulness* (Kandy : Buddhist Publication Society, 1967), pp. 10-15, 116-46; Vism. Chap. xviii; Nina Van Gorkom, *Buddhist Outlook on Daily Life* (Bangkok, 1969), pp. 56-69; Nina Van Gorkom, *Mental Development in Daily Life* (n.d.), pp. 92-246.

10. According to the Theravāda tradition a Buddha can experience physical pain, but he is completely free from all mental suffering. Besides the scriptural passage cited, *see* MA.ii.175.

11. There are two references to such a prediction in the Theravāda scriptures. The first is Buddha's warning to Devadatta that if he persisted in his schism he would go to hell (B.D.v.278). The second is Buddha's announcement to the monks of Devadatta's fate when he persisted in his schism (A.iv. 160; B.D.v.284). It is not stated that Devadatta was among the monks who heard this announcement but we can gather that the news would have reached him and that it would have upset him.

12. The commentary notes that Gotama remembered this period of time while he exhaled one breath (SA.iii.106).

13. Vism.xiv.133. For an excellent discussion of this topic, *see* Nina Van Gorkom, (1969), pp. 45-55.

Chapter Two

1. In a similar vein the monks Yamaka and Kaccāna praise the monks Sāriputta and Ānanda for being sympathetic and teaching them (S.iii.115, 315).

2. The householder's loving physical, verbal and mental activities will be discussed below in the section on loving activities (p. 34).

3. *kāruṇika* at M.ii.100, and *Kāruññataṃ paṭicca* at M.i.169 and S.i.138.

4. D.i.4; ii.212, 222, M.i.23, 46, 118, 121, 392; ii.238; iii.302; S.i.110, 111, 206; iv.322-25, 359, 361, 373; A.i.22; iii.5-6, 49, 87, 89; iv.139.

5. *appanāsamādhīnaṃ pubbabhāge* (Vism.iii.6).

6. The fourfold instructions for developing the sublime attitudes (*brahama-vihāra*) of love, compassion, sympathetic joy and equanimity occur at D.i.251; ii.186, 250; iii.50, 78, 224; M.i.38, 283-84, 297, 335, 351, 369; ii.76, 195, 207; iii.146; S.iv.296, 322; v.116; A.i.183, 192, 196; ii.128, 130, 184; iii.225; v.299-300, 344-45. In these instructions love and compassion are said to be cultivated in association with a "measureless" (*appamāṇa*) mind. The "measureless" mind is at the level of absorption, and the love that occurs therein is at the same level. (*See* Harvey B. Aronson, "Love, Compassion, Sympathetic Joy and Equanimity in Theravada Buddhism" [Ph.D. dissertation, University of Wisconsin, 1975], pp. 66-76).

Love and compassion are discussed as liberations of the mind (*cetovimutti*) at D.iii.247-48, 280; S.v.119-21; A.i.38, 42; iii.291; v.360, 360-61. The qualification "liberation of the mind" indicates that love and compassion at the level of at least the first absorption are meant (DA.ii.405-60).

"Love" and "compassion" appear as the objects of various forms of the verb "cultivate" (*bhāveti*) at M.i.424 (where they are said to mean access or placement love and compassion, according to MA.iii.140); at M.iii.81-82 (without comment); at A.iii.185 (where they are said to mean placement love and compassion, according to AA.iii.294); at S.v.131 (where they are said to mean placement love and compassion, according to SA.iii.176); at A.iii. 445-46 (just love, without comment). From the general commentarial pattern that emerges from the above commented-upon examples, it can be assumed that the uncommented-upon instances of "love" and "compassion" as objects of the verb "cultivate" refer to these attitudes at the level of access or placement.

"Love" appears alone, qualified as "measureless," or as a "liberation of the mind," or as occurring in a "measureless" mind, at M.i.127; A.iv.390; S.ii.264, 265; v.105; A.i.4; iv.150. "Measureless love," or "love" occurring in a "measureless" mind, both refer to love at the level of at least the first absorption. (*See* Aronson, pp. 66-76).

"Love" and "compassion" are unqualified at A.i.42 (where they can be understood to refer to placement love and compassion, according to the model of S.v.119-20, discussed at SA.iii.172-73, and Aronson, 312-23). "Love" is unqualified at A.i.26 (here it can be understood to refer to love at absorption according to Vism.xii.30-35). "Love" is unqualified at A.iii.443 (here "love" metaphorically refers to insight, AA.iii.415. This is discussed in the section on love in the present work, pp. 39-40). "Love" is unqualified at S.i.208 (it can be understood to refer to access or placement, as it is said to be "cultivated" love in the commentary, SA.i.305).

The unqualified neuter "love" (*metta*) appears once in the discourses at A.ii.72-73, where instructions are given on relating (*pharituṃ*) to snakes with love. No level of concentration is specifically prescribed.

"Compassion" appears in apposition to the term "absorption" (*jhāna*) at D.ii.237.

The masculine or neuter "compassion" (*karuṇa*) appears once at A.iii. 371-73 in the phrase *karuṇe vimuttā*, "liberated in compassion." This, no doubt, is the equivalent of compassion at the level of at least the level of the first absorption, when it is a "liberation of the mind."

Out of all the instances of "love" and "compassion" in the discourses, the only ones that are not clearly related to love and compassion at the level of access or placement are A.ii.72-73, where the neuter "love" (*metta*) occurs, and A.iii.443 (where "love" metaphorically refers to insight).

7. For the definitions of love and compassion, see Pa.ii.128, and Vism.ix.93-94. These will be discussed below in the section on the sublime attitudes (p. 63). Compare these definitions with the diffuse definitions of sympathy at DA.ii.456 and SA.ii.169, discussed above in the section on sympathy (p. 3).

8. The present work primarily concerns itself with the first four collections of discourses, their commentaries, and *The Path of Purification.* It does not attempt to deal systematically with the material in the fifth collection of discourses, the basket of discipline (*vinaya-piṭaka*), or the basket of higher-doctrine (*abhidhamma-piṭaka*) in the Theravāda canon. It should be noted, however, that the commentary to the higher-doctrine text *Compendium of Phenomena* (*Dhammasaṅgaṇi*) states that sympathy, along with several other fraternal attitudes, means access or placement love. "... *mettī* ...

anukampā sabbehi pi imehi padehi upacārappaṇappattā mettā ca vuttā."Buddhaghoṣa, *The Atthasālinī*; *Buddhaghosa's Commentary on the Dhammasaṅgaṇi*, ed. Edward Miller (London : Pali Text Society, 1897), p. 362. It must be kept in mind that this statement is from a commentary to a higher-doctrine work as opposed to a commentary on a discourse. This interpretation, which may serve the purpose of economy of concept in the higher-doctrine commentaries, in no way alters the fact that the discourses use "sympathy" in a non-technical way, and that their commentaries also do. Differences of opinion between commentaries are not uncommon. (*See* L. R. Goonesekere, *Buddhist Commentarial Literature*, The Wheel Publication, no. 113/114 [Kandy : Buddhist Publication Society, 1967], p. 21).

9. Two instances when it does occur in discourses on meditation are at M.i.127, and A.iv.150-1 (translated below, pp. 29, 57).

10. D.i.204; ii.133, and other references in *PTC*, I part iii.138.

11. For similar instructions by Sāriputta, *see* D.iii.211.

12. "Openness of mind" (*cetaso vivaraṃ*) occurs on those occasions when the mind is accompanied by serenity (*samatha*) or insight (*vipassanā*, AA.iii.295). "Clarity of Mind" (*cetaso pasādaṃ*) is the clarity of confidence (AA.iii.295).

13. Mindfulness only occurs in association with a wholesome mind (Vism. xiv.133, 156-58).

14. *kaṇhasukkadhammānaṃ yuganandhatā n'atthīti*, DAT.ii.398. English paraphrase at Soma-Thera p. 118.

15. Nyanaponika-Thera, *The Five Mental Hindrances*, 2nd ed. The Wheel Publication, no. 26 (Kandy : Buddhist Publication Society, 1961), ii.

16. I am indebted to Professor Jeffrey Hopkins of the University of Virginia for pointing this out.

17. Though an acquaintance with modern psychology would make one aware that the above-mentioned technique for displacing unwholesomeness is akin to "suppression" in the psychoanalytic sense, the physical and mental ease that would result from the above-mentioned technique mark it as distinct from any "suppression" that entails physical or mental discomfort.

The Theravādins also have a technical term "suppression" (*vikkhambhana*) but restrict its usage to the sustained, yet nevertheless temporary, abandonment of the defilements that occurs for the duration of absorption (Vism.xxii. 111). This suppression is not accompanied by any mental or physical stress. On the contrary, during absorption, the practitioner would enjoy the feelings of either bliss or equanimity (Vism.xiv.86). (For more on the temporary abandonment of the defilements through suppression, *see* Ledi-Sayadaw, *The Manual of Insight*, trans. U Nyāṇa Mahāthera, The Wheel Publication, no. 31/2 [Kandy : Buddhist Publication Society, 1961], pp. 79-82).

It is important to note that one does not need the sustained strength of absorption to displace unwholesome states of mind. Displacement of unwholesome states by wholesome states can be accomplished by an unconcentrated state of mind. This process is technically called "abandonment [through displacement] by its opposite" (*tadaṅga-pahāna*) (Vism.i.12). Since an unwholesome mind cannot coexist with a wholesome mind, turning the mind to a wholesome activity causes it to immediately displace the unwholesome state. (*See* Nyanaponika [1961], p. 4, and note 14 above). It is this type of unconcentrated displacement that is being referred to in this discourse passage. Though it is true that after much repeated practice one might be able to sustain the abandonment of defilements and deepen one's concentration, it is noteworthy that the process of abandoning hostility is effectively begun by an unconcentrated mind.

18. There are only five instances of this term in the first four collections of discourses — M.i.167-69; S.i.136-38; ii.199-200; A.iii.192-96; iv.186-90.

19. In the discourses, tender care is not associated with a specific meaning or a specific strength of mind. The exegesis of "the condition of tender care" (*anuddayatā*) as the sublime attitude sympathetic joy at SA.iii.227 is dictated by the unique context of S.v.168-69 (*see* pp. 53-55).

20. *See* note 18.

21. *The Pāṭimokha*, trans. Ñāṇamoli-Thera (Bangkok : Social Science Association Press, 1966), pp. 82-83.

22. *See* Chapter Six, note 30.

Chapter Three

1. On the levels and usage of "love" *see* above pp. 15-17, and Chapter Two, note 6. The analysis of love into three levels is not found in explicit form in the first four collections of discourses. According to the *Pali Tipiṭakam Concordance*, the word "access" (*upacāra*) does not occur at all in the first four collections of discourses and the word "placement" (*appanā*) occurs only once. On *upacāra see* *PTC.*, I part vii.392. On *appanā see PTC.*, I part iv.199, and M.iii.73.

2. For similar instructions *see* A.iii.196-98, 244.

3. *PTSD.*, pp. 114-15.

4. *See also* A.iv.104-105, where the material in this discourse is repeated with regard to the earlier teacher Sunetta, who is not specifically identified as the Bodhisattva.

5. For similar discussions *see* M.i.322-23; ii.250-51; A.iii.288-89.

6. *DAT.*, 169.

7. There are thirteen mental factors that accompany any wholesome mind: confidence (*saddhā*), mindfulness (*sati*), conscience (*hiri*), shame (*ottapam*), nongreed (*alobho*), nonhate [or love] (*adoso*), even-mindedness (*tatramajjhattatā*), tranquility of mind and body (*passaddhi*), lightness of mind and body (*lahutā*), flexibillity of mind and body (*mudutā*), efficiency of mind and body (*kammaññutā*), proficiency of mind and body (*pāguññatā*), straightforwardness of mind and body (*ujjukatā*) (Vism.xiv.133, 156-68). Cultivating any one of these thirteen will bring the other twelve (*see* for example Vism.iii.122). Thus, the practitioner with a mind endowed with love would have the twelve other wholesome mental factors that always accompany a wholesome mind. *See* above pp. 9-10 and Chapter One, note 8.

8. A wholesome mind endowed with love outside of the context of absorption would yield the benefits mentioned on pp. 24-28. If the practitioner cultivates his love to the level of absorption then his loving mind would yield the benefits discussed below on pp. 56-59.

Chapter Four

1. *See* Chapter Two, note 19.

2. At A.iii.445, love is said to have the same power in relation to hate (*dosa*). At S.v.105, love is said to be the opposite of the nutriment necessary for the arising and sustaining of anger.

3. The "hindrances" (*nīvaraṇa*) are the attitudes that are particularly obstructive to the attainment of the helpful state of absorption (Vism.iv.104). These attitudes are sense desire, anger, sloth and torpor, agitation and worry, and doubt.

4. On greedy states of mind and their association with agitation, *see* above pp. 6-7, and Vism.xiv.159-69. On agitation *see* Vism.xiv.165, and *DAT*. 2: 420. I am thankful to Professor Padmanabh S. Jaini of the University of California, Berkeley, for clarifying to me the relationship between attachment and agitation.

5. The commentary to the *Minor Readings* (*Khuddakapāṭha*), a work in the fifth collection of discourses, states that an enemy is a barrier, *sīmā nāma paccatthiko vuccati* (KP., 248). Thus breaking down the barriers means turning one's enemies into recipients of love.

6. *See* Chapter Two, note 14.

7. Nyanaponika-Thera (1961), p. 4.

8. *See* Chapter Two, note 17 and above pp. 40-41.

9. Eugene W. Burlingame, *Buddhist Legends : Translated from the Original Pali of the Dhammapada Commentary*. Harvard Oriental Series, vol. 28 (London : Pali Text Society, 1969), pp. 288-91.

10. This is the only instance in the first four collections of discourses in which the term "love" is a neuter noun (*metta*). The conditions for successful protection through the recitation and contemplation of this text are set out in *Milinda's Questions* (Miln., 154). This is a non-canonical text from the early Christian era. It states that the practitioner must be free of [past] obstructive karma, that he must be free of obstruction due to defilements (*kilesa*) [in the present], and that he must have confidence (*saddhā*).

11. The discourses do, however, state that the practitioner who cultivates the liberation of the mind which is love would be dear to humans (A.iv.150; for compassion and sympathetic joy, *see* Vism.ix.63, 83, 87). From this, we can understand that such a practitioner's over-all concern, balance, and peacefulness would be reassuring and quieting to others. His conduct and demeanor would endear him to them.

12. *See* D.iii. 248; 280; A.iii. 290-92; and Vism.ix. 93-95.

13. At first the commentary interprets the last three attitudes to mean love, compassion, and sympathetic joy *along with* their preliminary levels of development. The explanation of "harmlessness" (*avihimsā*) as compassion, along with the preliminary level of compassion is also to be found at SA.i. 355-56. The explanation of "the condition of tender care" as "sympathetic joy" is unique to this discourse. Otherwise "tender care" is not a technical term (see Chapter Two, note 19).

As was stated above (p. 15), the phrase "preliminary level" can refer either to the rudimentary or access level of concentration (above, p. 15). We need not decide which it means in the present situation since the inclusion of the preliminary levels in the above definitions is to show the theoretical strengths of love, and so forth. In the actual explanation of the passage at hand the terms love, and so on, are restricted in meaning to absorption states.

14. The whole commentary of this discourse, with minor variations, can be found at Vism.ix.60-76. Like the commentary to the "Smaller Snap," this commentary establishes that there are in theory three strengths of love (*see* above, p. 25). Here the weakest strength of love is "the strong state of mind [wishing] for [another's] welfare" (*balavahitacittatā*). This elaboration serves a heuristic purpose in the present context. What is actually the main topic in this commentary is love as a liberation of the mind — namely, placement love. It should be remembered that when "love" and "compassion" are used in the discourses, they are always said to be occurring at the level of access or placement, according to the commentaries. (*See* Chapter Two, note 6).

15. *PTSD*, p. 656.

16. *The Path of Purification* lists these two ways of abandoning defilements, along with "abandonment [through] displacement by its opposite," as the three ways of abandoning defilements (Vism.i.12; xxii.110-23). There are two other "abandonments" discussed in the commentaries. The first is "the abandonment in tranquillity" (*paṭipassadhipahānaṃ*), which refers to the absence of defilement in the mind at the time of fruition. The second is "the abandonment which is the escape" (*nissaraṇapahānam*) — namely, nirvāṇa, which is the escape from cyclic existence and is completely free of all defilement (MA.i.23). (*See also* Chapter Two, note 17).

17. On the level of strength of "measureless love" see Chapter Two, note 6.

18. This technique is discussed at MA.i.176 and in elaborate detail in Vism. chap.xviii-xxii. *See*, pp. 74-77.

19. The whole commentary to this discourse can be found at AA.v.82-83 and Vism.ix.60-76.

Chapter Five

1. "World of Brahman" (*Brahmaloka*) can refer to t he world of Brahma (neuter), or Brahmā (masculine). On the former, *see* Bṛh. 4.3.19-32; on the latter, *see* Kau.1.1-7. When one goes to the world of Brahman (masculine or neuter) one attains immortality. On attaining the world of Brahma (neuter), *see* Bṛh.6.2.15 (as opposed to Bṛh.4.4.4.), and Cha.8.4.1. On attaining the world of Brahmā (masculine), *see* Kau.1.1.-7. *See also* the discussion in Aronson, pp. 13-16. When one attains the world of Brahma or Brahmā one shares their status (*see* Bṛh.4.4.7; Kau.1.6.-7).

2. In the Buddhist discourses "Brahmā" is always masculine; the neuter "Brahma" does not appear. This usage might be related to the usage in the "Kauśītaki Upaniṣad," where "Brahmā" combines aspects that later are exclusively ascribed to either "Brahma" or "Brahmā" (*see* Aronson, pp. 17-22). According to Gotama, the world of Brahmā is populated by more than one Brahmā deity (D.i.245). Rebirth in the world of Brahmā does not give immortality (D.i.18; and below pp. 71-73).

3. After some time and the teachings of another discourse, these young men were sufficiently mature to cultivate insight. They did so and became Worthy Ones (DA.ii.406).

4. Gotama had already counseled the young men to give up the un-Brahmā-like hindrances (D.i.246). Here, he is stating the standard set of preparations necessary for concentration, the last step of which is the abandonment of the hindrances (D.i.250). For the purpose of giving the complete progression of practice up to concentration, this abandonment is mentioned again here.

5. According to the discourses and commentaries, an individual could practice meditation without becoming a monk or a nun, as the existence of practicing laymen and laywomen is recorded (for example, A.iv.208-235). In one discourse Gotama teaches the village headman Asibandhakaputta the unique meditations leading to communion with Brahmā, making no mention of the necessity for him to become a monk (S.iv.317-22). The only preliminary practice he taught him was correct conduct.

6. Whereas the sublime attitude equanimity is a contextually qualified form of even-mindedness, the feeling equanimity is not. (*see* below, pp. 81-85).

7. *The Ultimate Light* (*Paramatthajotikā*) is the commentary to the *Suttanipāta*, which is a work in the fifth collection of discourses.

8. *See* Chapter Two, note 6.

9. The present study is restricted to sympathy, love and the sublime attitudes. I would not like to leave the impression, however, that there are no teachings on social action apart from the teachings on the *motivations* for social action. Of note is K. S.iii.45-46, where laymen are urged to plant trees, build dams, dig wells and offer shelter to the homeless. It can be assumed that the first three activities were to be done for the good of the community at large; the last, clearly so. This injunction is discussed in Emanuel Sarkisyanz, *Buddhist Backgrounds of the Burmese Revolution* (The Hague : Martinus Nijhoff, 1964), p. 41. Also of note is D.i.135-36, where rulers are counseled to offer their subjects material assistance. This is discussed in A. K. Warder, *Indian Buddhism* (Delhi : Motilal Banarsidass, 1970), pp. 148-76. For several canonical prescriptions to laypersons on various helpful social activities, *see* Walpola Rahula, *The Heritage of the Bhikkhu*, pp. 3-7.

10. Sadness occurs only in association with aversive states of mind (Vism.xiv.92). If sadness arises when a practitioner is cultivating compassion, it indicates that his mind has changed from the wholesome state of wishing that another be free from suffering to the unwholesome state of aversion toward another's suffering. This is a fine but experientiable distinction.

11. Equanimity is specifically said to be the "escape" (*nissaraṇa*) from lust (*rāga*, D.iii.248, 280; A.iii.290-92).

12. Each of the first three sublime attitudes can be cultivated in any of the first three absorptions (Vism.ix.111). They are associated with bliss in these states (Vism.ix.111). On the bliss of the first three absorptions, *see* Vism.iv. 79, 139, 153. On the grossness of bliss as compared to the feeling equanimity, *see* Vism.iv.181.

13. At least one commentary states that love should be cultivated at the level of the first absorption, compassion at the level of the second, sympathetic joy at the level of the third, and equanimity at the level of the fourth (AA. iii.126). Following this progression, a practitioner would achieve skill in all of the first three sublime attitudes before cultivating equanimity. One has to be fully skilled in the first three absorptions before one can appreciate the subtle constituents of the fourth absorption, and know how to make them manifest (Vism.iv.131-32, 181-97).

14. In commenting on the same *sutta* passage occurring in the Middle Length Sayings Buddhaghoṣa adds at this point, "With regard to this, the activity of the sublime attitudes is considered to be included just among these [measureless activities of the form realm] (MA.iii.450).

15. *See* Chapter Two, note 6.

16. Out of the various canonical uses of "equanimity" (*see* Chapter Six, passim), the qualification stated here refers only to equanimity as a sublime attitude (Vism.iv.155-66).

17. The mental factors love, compassion, sympathetic joy and equanimity are called the sublime attitudes when they are cultivated according to the method of the fourfold instructions (Vism.ix.105). The states of mind in which these attitudes occur are also called the sublime attitudes. Thus, when MA.iii.450 says "activity of the sublime attitudes" (*brahmavihārakamma* [*see* above, nt. 14]), it is referring to the intention in *the mind* which is endowed with cultivated love, or one of the other attitudes.

18. Each of the sublime attitudes will give the eleven benefits mentioned in association with the cultivation of love (*see* above pp. 56, 59; *see also* Vism.ix.59-76, 83, 87, 90).

19. *See* note 18 above.

20. The Bodhisattva in earlier lives as Mahāsudassana (D.ii.146-47), Jotipāla (D.ii.250), and Makhādeve (M.ii.76) cultivated the four sublime attitudes according to the method of the fourfold instructions. In addition, ancient Brahmins were said to teach the absorption which is compassion (*karunaṃ jhānaṃ*) (D.ii.237).

21. *See* S.v.410 in conjunction with DA.iii.992.

22. *See also* MLS.ii.378, note 1.

23. In practice the sublime attitudes can be cultivated before or after one cultivates insight. What is important to remember is that these attitudes are not the whole practice, or the most important practice, on the Buddhist path. They complement the teachings on sympathy, conduct, and insight.

24. The "knowledgeable disciple of the noble ones" (*sutavata ariyasâvakassa*, A.ii.128-29) is identified as a Stream-Enterer (or higher) at S.v.363. A Stream-Enterer's realization is such that he no longer believes in a permanent personality, no longer clings to empty rites, and no longer is bothered by religious doubt (Vism.xxii.64). In addition, because of his realization, he has forever abandoned the propensity to certain types of rebirth. He will never again be reborn as a hell being, a hungry ghost, or as an animal. In contrast to normal intentions, which condition an individual to a good or bad fate, the intention that occurs at the time that nirvāṇa is realized deconditions the mind so that it becomes free of certain fates. The Stream-Enterer

has become free from low rebirth; the Worthy One, from all rebirth. On the process of deconditioning, *see* A.ii.230-38 and a wonderful piece of Buddhadasa's in his *Buddha Dhamma for Students,* trans. Ariyananda Bhikkhu (Bangkok : Sublime Life Mission, 1966), pp. 20-23. This is available upon request from the Sublime Life Mission, V. Siriath f/1 Atsadan Road, Bangkok, Thailand.

25. Love, compassion, sympathetic joy and equanimity are elsewhere said to be the "escapes" from anger, hostility, displeasure and lust (*see* above p. 63 and note 11). Though equanimity is said to be the "escapes" from lust, it clearly can oppose aversion as well (*see also*, Vims. ix.96).

26. *See* Chapter Two, note 17 and above, pp. 58-59.

27. Ānanda also teaches Dasama that he can use the above method with the other three sublime attitudes, or with the four form realm absorptions, or with the first three formless realm attainments (for similar instructions, *see* A.v.360-67). Since this discourse is addressed to a layman, it shows that at the time of the Buddha there were laypersons interested in the ultimate teachings and that they were instructed accordingly.

As there are several ways for achieving the form realm absorptions, such as meditating on earth-colored circles, and so forth, there are many ways for a practitioner to conjoin the cultivation of concentration and insight (Vism. iv.104-107; xviii.3). Though cultivation of the sublime attitudes to the level of form realm absorption can be conjoined with the practice of insight to lead to realization of nirvāṇa, this is not the only means. It is even possible to realize nirvāṇa without having cultivated access concentration or form realm absorption. (*See* Mahasi Sayadaw, *The Progress of Insight*, trans. Nyānaponika Thera [Kandy : Buddhist Publication Society, 1973], pp. 4-6). Whether a practitioner chooses to cultivate absorption first and then insight, or insight on the basis of less highly developed concentration will depend on his temperament and his teacher's advice (Vism.iii.74-130). Similar considerations would determine a meditator's timing for undertaking the cultivation of one or more of the sublime attitudes. The teacher's choice will depend on the student's interest and capacity at any given moment (*see* above, pp. 60, 72).

It should be noted, that whatever path a practitioner chooses will, at the least, include some cultivation of love as a preliminary practice (*see* above, p. 51).

28. For a full description of the cultivation of insight, *see* Vism. chap. xviii-xxii.

29. Buddhaghoṣācariya, *Visuddhimagga with Paramatthamañjūsāṭīkā of Bhadantācariya Dhammapāla*, ed. Rewatadhamma, 3 Vols. (Varanasi : Varanaseya Sanskrit Vishvavidyalaya), 3:1512, commentary section 3; also, P.P.xxi.4.nt.3.

30. *Ibid.*

Chapter Six

1. King, pp. 161-168; Spiro, pp. 47-48.
2. King, pp. 138-175; Spiro, pp. 29-139.
3. King, pp. 161-168.

4. *Ibid.*, p. 168.
5. *Ibid.*, p. 162.
6. Weber is cited in Spiro, p. 427.
7. *Ibid.*, p. 427.
8. *Ibid.*, p. 48.
9. Spiro indicates that the practitioner cultivates "detachment" once he has proceeded through love, compassion and sympathetic joy (Spiro, p. 48). It is thus clear that he is referring to the standard progressive development of the sublime attitudes, and that "detachment" here refers specifically to the sublime attitude equanimity.
10. H. Saddhatissa, *Buddhist Ethics* (New York : George Braziller, 1970), p. 68.
11. In works of higher knowledge (*abhidhamma*) such intentions are called "functional" (*kriyā*) — they work in the present but produce no effect in the future. Fully liberated beings produce intentions which are similar in character to the wholesome intentions of worldly individuals, differing from the latter in that they do not entail rebirth. *See* Nārada Mahāthera, ed. and trans., *A Manual of Abhidhamma : Being Abhidhammattha Sangaha* (Kandy : Buddhist Publication Society, 1968), pp. 22, 35-39; Vism. xiv.109.
12. Unlike the mundane absorption states which have the counterpart sign (Vism.iv.31, 181) or sentient beings as their objects, the mind realizing nirvāṇa is considered supramundane because of its object.
13. The individual being described here is identified as fully liberated at AA.iii.335.
14. Buddhaghoṣācariya, *Visuddhimagga with Paramatthamañjūsāṭīkā of Bhaddantācariya Dhammapāla*, 2:682, commentary sec. 72.
15. Aronson, pp. 268-276.
16. It must be reemphasized here that in order to realize nirvāṇa one need not cultivate any of the sublime attitudes to absorption (*See* Chapter Five, note 27). Furthermore any one of the sublime attitudes can serve as a basis for the realization of nirvāṇa (*see* above, p. 75). If, however, a meditator's practice included cultivation of the four sublime attitudes, the sublime attitude equanimity would be the most potent for producing the limb of enlightenment equanimity.
17. King, p. 161.
18. *Ibid.*, pp. 161-162.
19. AA.iii.126; Vism.ix.88; Buddhaghoṣācariya, *Visuddhimagga with Paramatthamañjūsāṭīkā of Bhaddhantācariya Dhammapāla*, 2:672, commentary sec. 63.
20. *See also*, Vism.ix.108.
21. King, p. 162.
22. *Ibid.*
23. *See* for example the "Siṅgālovāda Suttanta, "D.iii.180-193.
24. Even the practitioner's temporary cultivation of the neutral sublime attitude equanimity should be motivated by his understanding of his practice's benefit for others — his exemplification of a restful state and, with mastery of it, his ability to teach others how to achieve it.

25. Henry Clarke Warren, trans., *Buddhism : In Translations* (New York : Atheneum, 1963), pp. 5-15.

26. *Ibid.*

27. *Ibid.*

28. A. K. Warder, *Indian Buddhism* (Delhi : Motilal Banarsidass, 1970), p. 218.

29. King, p. 162.

30. *See*, Soma-Thera, *The Way of Mindfulness : The Satipaṭṭhāna Sutta and Commentary* (Kandy : Buddhist Publication Society, 1967), pp. 144-45. It should be noted here that any neutrality towards beings outside the context of the fourth absorption would not constitute the sublime attitude equanimity. It would be the preliminary aspect of the sublime attitude equanimity and technically would fall into the category of even-minded equanimity. *See* Aronson, pp. 263-282, and P.P.ix.nt. 20.

31. Professor David Little of the University of Virginia has suggested this line of argumentation.

32. Lecture given in Dalhousie, India, October 1972.

33. AA.i.69-70; Henry Clarke Warren, pp. 91-95.

34. *See* for example the anecdotes in Vism.i.55, 105-120 and the biographical material throughout Walpola Rahula's, *History of Buddhism in Ceylon* (Colombo : M. D. Gunasena), 1956.

35. King, pp. 162, 168.

36. *See* for example the "Sāmaññaphala Suttanta" (D.i.47-86), or the "Kūṭadanta Suttanta" (D.i.127-149).

37. *See* for example Walpola Rahula's, *The Heritage of the Bhikkhu*, passim.

38. Spiro, p. 48.

39. When one attains the path consciousness which realizes nirvāṇa one abandons defilements for ever (Vism.xxii.122). At this time all seven limbs of enlightenment would be present. It is a distortion to separate out the limb of enlightenment equanimity from the other limbs which are equally important for this process. However, in so far as Spiro has focused attention on "detachment"/*upekkhā*/[equanimity], and I am trying to unravel the etiology of his usage, I have singled out the limb of enlightenment equanimity (*bojjhaṅga-upekkhā*) for mention here.

40. The sublime attitude equanimity itself does not have the ability to permanently destroy negative attitudes, though it does have the capacity to suppress them temporarily (Vism.xxii.111).

41. Witness the exemplary model of the Buddha (*see* above, p. 73 and A.1.180-185).

BIBLIOGRAPHY

A. *Works Cited by Abbreviation*

Unless stated otherwise all the works listed below have been published in London by the Pali Text Society.

A. *Aṅguttara Nikāya.* Ed. Richard Morris. I, 2nd ed., 1961. II, 1888; rpt., 1955. Ed. E. Hardy. III, 1897; rpt., 1958. IV, 1899; rpt., 1958. V, 1900; rpt., 1958.

AA. Buddhaghosa. *Manorathapūraṇī : Buddhaghosa's Commentary on the Aṅguttara Nikāya.* Ed. Max Walleser. I, 1924. Ed. Herman Kopp. II, 2nd ed., 1967. III, 1936; rpt., 1966. IV, 1940; rpt., 1963. V, 1946.

B.D. *Book of the Discipline.* Trans. I. B. Horner. V, 1963.

Bṛh. "Bṛhadāraṇyaka Upaniṣad," in *The Principal Upaniṣads.* Ed. S. Radhakrishnan. London : George Allen and Unwin Ltd., 1969, pp. 147-333.

Cha. "Chāndogya Upaniṣad," in *The Principal Upaniṣads.* Ed. S. Radhakrishnan. London : George Allen and Unwin Ltd., 1969, pp. 335-51a.

D. *Dīgha Nikāya.* Eds. T. W. Rhys Davids and J. Estlin Carpenter. I, 1890; rpt., 1967. II, 1903; rpt., 1966. Ed. J. Estlin Carpenter. III, 1911; rpt., 1960.

DA. *Sumaṅgala-vilāsanī : Buddhaghosa's Commentary on the Dīgha Nikāya.* Eds. T. W. Rhys Davids and J. Estlin Carpenter. I, 2nd ed., 1968. Ed. W. Stede III, 2nd ed. 1971. III, 2nd ed., 1971.

DAT. Dhammapāla. *Dīghanikāyaṭṭhakathāṭikālīnatthavaṇṇanā.* Ed. Lily De Silva. II, 1970.

Exp. *The Expositor (Atthasālinī) : Buddhaghosa's Commentary on the Dhammasangaṇī The First Book of the Abhidhamma Piṭaka.* Trans. Pe Maung Tin. Ed. C.A.F. Rhys Davids. I, 1920; rpt., 1958. II, 1921; rpt., 1958.

K. S. *The Book of the Kindred Sayings (Saṁyutta Nikāya).* Trans. F. L. Woodward. V, 1927; rpt., 1972. V, 1930; rpt., 1965.

Kau. "Kauśītaki Upaniṣad," in *The Principal Upaniṣads.* Ed. W. Radhakrishnan. London : George Allen and Unwin Ltd., 1969, pp. 751-791.

KP. *Khuddaka-Pāṭha. Together with its Commentary Paramatthajotikā I.* Ed. Elmer Smith, 1915.

M. *Majjhima Nikāya.* Ed. V. Trenckner. I, 1888; rpt., 1964. Ed. Robert Chalmers. II, 1898; rpt., 1960. III, 1899; rpt., 1960.

MA. *Papañcasudanī : Buddhaghosa's Commentary on the Majjhima Nikāya.* Eds. J. H. Woods and D. Kosambi. I, 1924. II, 1925, Ed. I. B. Horner. III, 1933. IV, 1937. V, 1938.

M.L.S. *The Collection of Middle Length Sayings (Majjhima Nikāya). Trans. I. B. Horner.* II, 1957; rpt., 1970.

Miln. *The Milindapañho.* Ed. V. Trenckner, 1880; rpt., 1962.

P.P. Buddhaghosa. *Path of Purification (Visuddhimagga).* Trans. Bhikkhu Ñyāṇamoli. 2nd ed. Colombo : A. Semage, 1964.

PTC. *Pāli Tipiṭakam Concordance.* Ed. E. M. Hare. I Part III, 1953. I Part IV, 1954. I Part VII, 1955. II Part I, 1956.

PTSD. *The Pali Text Society's Pali-English Dictionary* 1921-5; rpt., 1972.

Pa. *Sutta Nipāta Commentary Being Paramatthajotikā.*, 1916.

S. *Saṁyutta Nikāya.* Ed. Leon M. Feer. I, 1884. II, 1888; rpt., 1970. III, 1890; rpt., 1960. IV, 1894. V, 1898; rpt., 1960.

SA. Buddhaghosa. *Sāratthappakāsinī : Buddhaghosa's Commentary on the Saṁyutta Nikāya.* Ed. F. L. Woodwards. I, 1929. II, 1932. III, 1937.

Vin. *The Vinaya Piṭaka.* Ed. H. Oldenberg. III, 1881; rpt., 1964.

Vism. Buddhaghosa. *Visuddhimagga.* Ed. Henry Clark Warren. Harvard Oriental Series, 41. Cambridge : Harvard University Press, 1950.

B. *Works Cited by Title*

Dialogues of the Buddha (Dīgha Nikāya). Trans. T. W. Rhys Davids and C. A. F. Rhys Davids. I, 1899; rpt., 1956. II, 4th ed., 1959. III, 1921; rpt. London : Pali Text Society, 1957.

The Book of the Gradual Sayings (*Aṅguttara Nikāya*). Trans. F. L. Woodward. I, 1932; rpt., 1970. II, 1933; rpt., 1973. Trans. E. M. Hare. III, 1934; rpt., 1973. IV, 1935; rpt., 1965. V, 1936; rpt. London : Pali Text Society, 1972.

The Book of the Kindred Sayings (*Saṁyutta Nikāya*). Trans. C. A. F. Rhys Davids. I, 1917; rpt., 1971. II, 1917; rpt., 1971. Trans. F. L. Woodward. III, 1925; rpt. 1954. IV. 1927; rpt., 1972. V, 1930; rpt. London : Pali Text Society, 1965.

The Middle Length Sayings (*Majjhima Nikāya*). Trans. I. B. Horner. I, 1954; rpt., 1967. II, 1957; rpt., 1970. III, 1959; rpt. London : Pali Text Society, 1967.

C. *Other Works*

Aronson, Harvey B. "Love, Compassion, Sympathetic Joy and Equanimity in Theravada Buddhism." Ph.D. dissertation, University of Wisconsin, 1975.

Buddhadasa, Bhikkhu. *Buddha Dhamma for Students.* Trans. Ariyananda Bhikkhu. Bangkok : Sublime Life Mission, 1966.

Buddhaghosa. *The Atthasālinī; Buddhaghosa's Commentary on the Dhammasaṅgaṇi.* Ed. Edward Miller. London : Pali Text Society, 1897.

Buddhaghosācariya. *Visuddhimaggo with Paramatthamañjūsāṭīkā of Bhadantācariya Dhammapāla.* Ed. Rewatadhamma, 3 vols. Varanasi : Varanaseya Sanskrit Vishvavidyalaya, 1969-72.

Burlingame, Eugene W. *Buddhist Legends : Translated from the Original Pali of the Dhammapada Commentary.* Harvard Oriental Series, 28. London : Pali Text Society, 1969.

Goonasekere, L. R. *Buddhist Commentarial Literature.* The Wheel Publication, 113. Kandy : Buddhist Publication Society, 1967.

Govinda, Lama Anagarika. *The Psychological Attitude of Early Buddhist Philosophy.* London : Rider and Company, 1969.

King, Winston. *In the Hope of Nibbana : Theravada Buddhist Ethics.* LaSalle : Open Court, 1964.

Ledi, Sayadaw. *The Manual of Insight*. Trans. U Nyāna Mahāthera. The Wheel Publication, 31/2. Kandy : Buddhist Publication Society, 1961.

Mahasi, Sayadaw. *Practical Insight Meditation*. San Francisco : Unity Press, 1972.

———. *The Progress of Insight*. Trans. Nyānaponika Thera. Kandy : Buddhist Publication Society, 1973.

Malalasekera, G. P. *Dictionary of Pali Proper Names*. 2 vols. London : Pali Text Society, 1969.

Nārada, Mahā Thera. *A Manual of Abhidhamma : Being Abhidhammattha Sangaha*. Kandy : Buddhist Publications Society, 1968.

Ñāṇamoli, Thera, trans. *The Pāṭimokha*. Bangkok : Social Science Association Press, 1966.

Nyanaponika, Thera. *The Five Mental Hindrances*. 2nd ed. The Wheel Publication, 26. Kandy : Buddhist Publication Society, 1961.

———. *The Heart of Buddhist Meditation*. London : Rider and Company, 1969.

———. *The Power of Mindfulness*. San Francisco : Unity Press, 1972.

Pusalker, A. D. "Religion and Philosophy : The Pali Canon," *History and Culture of the Indian People*. 2nd ed. general ed. R. C. Majumdar. Bombay : Bharatiya Vidya Bhavan, 1953, II : 396-409.

Rahula, Walpola. *History of Buddhism in Ceylon*. Colombo : M. D. Gunasena, 1956.

———. *The Heritage of the Bhikkhu : A Short History of the Bhikkhu in Educational, Cultural, Social and Political Life*. trans. K. P. G. Wijayasurendra. New York : Grove Press, 1974.

Rhys Davids, C. A. F. "Love (Buddhist)," in *Encyclopedia of Religion and Ethics*. Ed. James Hastings. New York : Charles Scribner's Sons, 1916, 8:159-62.

Saddhatissa, H. *Buddhist Ethics*. New York : George Braziller, 1970.

Sarkisyanz, Emanuel. *Buddhist Backgrounds of the Burmese Revolution*. The Hague : Martinus Nijhoff, 1964.

Soma, Thera. *The Way of Mindfulness*. Kandy : Buddhist Publication Society, 1967.

Spiro, Melford. *Buddhism and Society : A Great Tradition and Its Burmese Vicissitudes.* New York : Harper Paperbacks, 1972.

Swearer, Donald K. *Buddhism in Transition.* Philadelphia : Westminster Press, 1970.

Van Gorkom, Nina. *Buddhist Outlook on Daily Life.* Bangkok, 1969.

———. *Mental Development in Daily Life.* (n.d.)

Warder, A. K. *Indian Buddhism.* Delhi : Motilal Banarsidass, 1970.

Warren, Henry Clarke. *Buddhism : In Translations.* New York : Atheneum, 1963.

Weeraratne, W. G. "Anukampā," in *Encyclopedia of Buddhism.* Ed. G. P. Malalasekera. Government of Ceylon, 1967, fascicle 4:742.

ENGLISH-PALI GLOSSARY

abandoning defilements by uprooting them — *samuccheda-ppahāna*
abandoning defilements (temporarily) by displacing them — *tadaṅga-ppahāna*
abandoning defilements (temporarily) by suppressing them — *vikkhamabhana-ppahāna*
abandonment — *pahāna*
absorption — *jhāna*
abstinence from wrong activity — *kāyaduccaritavirati*
abstinence from wrong livelihood — *micchājīvavirati*
abstinence from wrong speech — *vacīduccaritavirati*
access concentration — *upacāra-samādhi*
act of knowing — *see* consciousness
adaptability — *kammaññutā*
agitation — *uddhacca*
alms food — *piṇḍa*
almsgiving — *dāna*
anger — *vyāpāda*
approval — *anunaya*
arising — *uppajjamāna*
attachment — *lobha, sineha*
attachment to rites and rituals — *silabbataparāmāsa*
attend — *paccupaṭṭhāpeti*
aversion — *paṭigha*
bad fate — *duggati*
balance — *majjhatta*
basket — *piṭaka*
benefit — *attha*
bliss — *sukha*
Brahmin — *Brāhmaṇa*
breaking down barriers — *sīmasambheda*
calm — *passaddha*
care — *anudayā*
cessation — *nirodha*
cause — *hetu*

clarity of mind — *cetaso pasāda*
clear minded — *pasādita-citta*
collection of discourses — *nikāya*
coming to be — *uppajjati*
communion — *sahavyatā*
compact mass — *samūha-ghana*
compassion — *karuṇā*
concentration — *samādhi*
condition — *paccaya*
conditioned phenomena — *saṅkhāra*
conditioning mental factor — *saṅkhāra*
confidence — *saddhā*
conscience — *hiri*
consciousness — *viññāṇa*
consume — *bhuñjati*
correct conduct — *sīla*
counterpart sign — *paṭibhāganimitta*
cultivate — *bhāveti*
cyclic existence — *saṃsāra*
danger — *ādinava*
decision — *adhimokkha*
defilements — *kilesa*
delusion — *moha*
dependent origination — *paṭicca samuppāda*
desire — *kāma*
desire for the form realm — *rūparāga*
desire for the formless realm — *arūparāga*
desire realm — *kāmāvacara*
desirous bias — *anurodha*
diffuse — *vyagga*
direct knowledge — *abhiññā*
discipline — *vinaya*
discourse — *sutta*
discrimination — *sampajāna*
dispassion — *virāga*
displacement — *see* abandoning defilements
dissatisfaction — *virodha*
displeasure — *arati*
distraction — *uddhacca, vikkhepa*
doubt — *vicikicchā*

efficiency — *kammaññutā*
eightfold noble path — *ariyo aṭṭhangiko maggo*
elder — *thera*
eliminative abandonment — *samuccheda-ppahāna*
energy — *viriya*
enlarged — *mahaggata*
enlightened — *buddha*
enlightenment — *bodhi, sambodhi*
enmity — *vera*
enjoy — *paribhuñjati*
envy — *issā*
equanimity — *upekkhā*
(a) equanimity of purity — *parisuddhi-upekkhā*
(b) even-minded equanimity — *tatra-majjhatta-upekkhā*
(c) feeling equanimity — *vedanā-upekkhā*
(d) limb of enlightenment equanimity — *bojjhaṅga-upekkhā*
(e) six-limbed equanimity — *chaḷaṅga-upekkhā*
(f) sublime attitude equanimity — *brahma-vihāra-upekkhā*
(g) unknowing equanimity — *aññāṇa-upekkhā*
escape — *nissaraṇa*
establishing — *upaṭṭhāpeti*
establishment of mindfulness — *satipaṭṭhāna*
even-minded — *majjhattabhāva*
fetters — *saṃyojana*
flexibility — *mudutā*
form realm — *rūpāvacara*
formless realm — *arūpāvacara*
Fortunate One — *Bhagavant*
foundation of cyclic existence — *upadhi*
freedom from bondage — *yogakkhema*
fruit, fruition — *phala*
fruition attainment — *phala samāpatti*
function — *rasa*
functional — *kriyā*
general characteristic — *sāmañña-lakkhaṇa*
generosity — *alobha, dāna*
gift giving — *dāna*
grasping — *gahaṇa*
greed — *lobha*
grief — *dummana*

happiness — *sukha*
harmful — *vihesāvant*
harmful influences — *āsava*
harmlessness — *avihiṃsā*
Harmonious One — *Tathāgata*
hatred — *dosa*
heaven — *sagga*
hell — *niraya*
higher knowledge — *abhidhamma*
hindrances — *nīvaraṇa*
hoarding — *macchariya*
hostility — *āghāta*
hungry ghost — *pitti, peta*
immortal — *amata*
ignorance — *avijjā*
impermanence — *anicca*
impure — *aparisuddha*
inclination to act — *chanda*
inherent tendencies — *anusaya*
initial application of mind to its object — *vitakka*
insight — *vipassanā*
investigation of phenomena — *dhamma-vicaya*
intention — *cetanā*
joy — *pāmujja*
kindness — *kalyāṇa-manas*
lack of conscience — *ahiri*
lack of shame — *anottappa*
layman — *upāsaka*
laywoman — *upāsikā*
liberated — *vimutta*
liberation — *vimokkha*
liberation of mind — *cetovimutti*
lightness — *lahutā*
love — *mettā*
loving — *metta*
loving mental activity — *mettaṃ mano-kammaṃ*
loving mind — *metta-citta*
loving physical activity — *mettaṃ kāya-kammaṃ*
loving verbal activity — *mettaṃ vacī-kammaṃ*
lunar observance day — *uposatha*

lust — *rāga*
material phenomena — *rūpa*
measured activity — *pamāṇakataṃ kammaṃ*
measureless — *appamāṇa*
meditation — *bhāvanā*
mental factor — *ceasika*
mental phenomena — *nāma*
mental pleasure — *somanassa*
mental suffering — *domanassa*
merit — *puñña*
merriment — *pahāsa*
mind — *citta*
mindfulness — *sati*
monk — *bhikkhu*
nirvāṇa — *nibbāna*
noble one — *ariya*
neutrality — *majjhatta*
noble truth — *ariyasacca*
Nonenlightening Buddha — *Pacceka Buddha*
nongreed — *alobha*
nonhate — *adosa*
nonhuman spirit — *amanussa*
Nonreturner — *Anāgamin*
nonvirtue — *akusala*
novice — *navaka*
nun — *bhikkhunī*
Once-Returner — *Sakadāgamin*
one who has destroyed the harmful influences — *khīṇāsava*
openness of mind — *cetaso vivara*
pain — *dukkha*
path — *magga*
path consciousness — *magga-citta*
patience — *khanti*
peace — *santa*
peak of existence — *bhavagga*
perception — *saññā*
Perfectly Enlightened One — *Sammāsambuddha*
placement concentration — *appanā samādhi*
placing — *appeti*
pleasure — *sukha*

pleasurable interest — *pīti*
practice — *dhamma*
preliminary level — *pubba-bhāga*
pride — *māna*
produced — *abhisaṅkhata*
proficiency — *pāguññatā*
profit — *attha*
protection — *anurakkhā*
pure — *parisuddha*
realize — *sacchikaroti*
rebirth, harmful influence with regard to — *bhava-āsava*
recluse, state of being a — *sāmañña*
relate — *pharati*
reliquary — *cetiya*
remorse — *vippaṭisara*
renunciation — *pabbajjā*
requisites — *parikkhāra*
restraint — *saññama*
right action — *sammā-kammanta*
right concentration — *sammā-samādhi*
right direction — *sammā-saṃkappa*
right effort — *sammā-vāyāma*
right livelihood — *sammā-ājīva*
right mindfulness — *sammā-sati*
right speech — *sammā-vācā*
right view — *sammā-diṭṭhi*
rudimentary level — *sabba-pubba-bhāga*
ruin — *vinipāta*
sadness — *soka, domanassa*
selfless — *anattā*
sense desire — *kāmarāga, kāmacchanda*
sentient being — *satta*
serenity — *samatha*
shame — *ottappa*
simple compassion — *kāruñña*
sloth — *thīna*
specific characteristics — *paccatalakkhaṇa*
spiritual community — *saṅgha*
state of loss — *apāya*
state of having a tender mind — *muducitta*

status consciousness — *māna*
straightforwardness — *ujukatā*
Stream-Enterer — *Sotāpatti*
sublime attitude — *brahma-vihāra*
suffering — *dukkha*
supramundane — *lokuttara*
suppressive abandonment — *vikkhambhana-ppahāna*
sustain — *āsevati*
sustained application of mind to its object — *vicāra*
sympathy — *anukampā*
sympathetic joy — *muditā*
tender — *muduka*
tender care — *anuddayā*
tender minded — *mudukatacitta*
Three Baskets — *Tepiṭaka*
torpor — *middha*
trainee — *sekha*
training — *sikhā*
tranquility — *passaddhi*
ultimate aim — *paramatthattha*
ultimate sense — *paramattha*
unwholesome — *akusala*
uproot—*samuccheda*
virtue — *kusala*
wanderer — *samaṇa*
welfare — *hita*
wholesome — *kusala*
wisdom — *paññā*
world — *loka*
world of Brahma — *Brahmaloka*
worry — *kukkucca*
Worthy One — *Arahant*
wrong view — *diṭṭhi*
wrong view of individuality — *sakkāyadiṭṭhi*

PROPER NAMES AND DISCOURSES

Cited by Name

INDEX